D0468263

THE WAY OF THE SPIRIT

THE WAY OF THE SPIRIT

TIME®
LIFE
BOOKS

Above: *Emblazoned on the center of this elk-skin robe is an emblem symbolizing war honors*

Left: *Cheyenne/Sioux powwow dancer summons the Spirit*

Previous page: *Concentric circles on a Gros Ventre warrior shield symbolizing the belief that all things in the universe are interconnected in a divine and harmonious fashion*

TIME-LIFE BOOKS IS A DIVISION OF TIME LIFE INC.

TIME-LIFE CUSTOM PUBLISHING

Vice President and Publisher	Terry Newell
Associate Publisher	Teresa Hartnett
Director of Editorial Development	Jennifer Pearce
Director of Sales	Neil Levin
Director of Special Sales	Liz Ziehl
Managing Editor	Donia Ann Steele
Director of Design	Christopher M. Register
Research	Kimberly A. Grandcolas

Designed and produced by Tehabi Books, Del Mar, California

Library of Congress Cataloging-in-Publication Data

The way of the spirit/ editors of Time-Life Books.

    p. cm.

    Includes biographical references and index.

    ISBN 0-7835-4908-3

    1. Spiritual life. 2. Indians of North America—Religion.

I. Time-Life Books.

BL624. W3833 1997

299' .7—dc21   96-48059

                                     CIP

Books produced by TIME-LIFE Custom Publishing are available
at special bulk discount for promotional and premium use.
Custom adaptations can also be created to meet your specific marketing goals.
Call 1-800-323-5255.

Right: *Ceremonial powwow dance bustle*

Above: *Bleached and painted buffalo skull used by the peoples of the Great Plains in the Sun Dance ceremony*
Left: *North Dakota Mandan shaman ritually lifts a buffalo skull skyward to ensure a successful hunt*

WITHIN THIS CIRCLE

According to traditional North American Indian thinking, there is nothing that can be seen or touched, living or inanimate, that does not have a spirit. As Lame Deer, a Lakota Sioux, explains: "We Indians live in a world of symbols where the spiritual and the commonplace are one. We try to understand them not with the head but with the heart, and we need no more than a hint to give us meaning."

A pipe or a pair of moccasins may appear quaint or mundane to non-Indian eyes but they may have enormous spiritual significance to an Indian. The dramas and songs, like the ceremonial dances, are not performed for entertainment, but for attainment of the Balanced Life. In this, they are the very essence of Indian life.

"All things are tied together with a common navel cord," as one Sioux elder

Above: *Southern Plains medicine shield trimmed in eagle feathers with bear claw design evoking physical and spiritual protection*
Left: *Thunderstorm over Monument Valley, Arizona*

explained. Everything that exists possesses a soul, and all of these souls are mutually dependent. Mysterious powers abide in all things—the flora, the fauna, the very earth itself. Native Americans believe that if they act in accordance with sacred tradition, they maintain harmony between humans and other elements of the natural world. If they violate the sacred ways, however, the orderly workings of the natural world are thrown out of kilter, and the imbalance may cause bad things to happen—sickness, accident, disaster.

Eighteenth-century quilled moccasins

For help in meeting the trials inherent in everyday life, Indians have traditionally appealed to the spirits of familiar creatures rather than supernatural ones. According to the lore of numerous tribes, each animal, from the tiny butterfly to the massive buffalo, possesses special powers or medicines which can be imparted to humans who understand and respect them. The butterfly, for instance, exemplifies elusiveness. Before setting off into battle, some Indian warriors painted their bodies with butterfly symbols to invoke the insect's power and protect them from the arrows and bullets of their enemies. It was believed that bear power could cure illness. Shamans or medicine men from many different groups—including the Sioux, the Chippewa, and the Pueblo peoples—frequently dressed as bears when working to heal the sick. Just as honoring the bear spirit could bring blessings to people, provoking the spirit might bring them harm. For that reason, some tribes, most notably the Apache, forbade their hunters to kill a bear or even to touch the carcass of one found dead in the woods. The killing of eagles, creatures that were revered as lords of the air, was outlawed in a number of Indian communities.

Sun Dance ceremonial robe with butterfly symbols

Since time immemorial, many Indians seeking assistance from an animal spirit have decorated their tools and weapons with a fetish, or emblem, of the creature's power. To many Indian peoples, particularly those of the Great Plains, the most important fetish was a collection of spiritually charged articles known as a medicine bundle. Still carried by some

10

Crow warrior buffalo hide shield

Indians today, each bundle consists of an array of charms—beads, stones, dried herbs, and the claws, teeth, or other parts of animals—wrapped in a pouch made from the skin of the creature with whom the bundle's owner has established a special relationship.

Traditionally, the selection of this skin, and of the objects in the bundle, would be revealed to the owner in a vision or dream. Many young men—as well as some young women—sought the animal spirit that would become their lifelong helper by going on a vision quest, the focal point of the religious life of most Native Americans, an ordeal that usually involved fasting and other forms of deprivation.

Mother Earth as life host, the relationship of reciprocity between human beings and animals, the Indian's dependence on animals as teachers—all of these reflect the view that human beings are no more important than any other thing, whether living or inanimate. In the eye of the Creator, man and woman, plant and animal, water and stone, all share the earth as equal partners—even as family. "We Indians think of the earth and the whole universe as a never-ending circle, and in this circle, man is just another animal," explains Jenny Leading Cloud of the Rosebud Indian Reservation. "The buffalo and the coyote are our brothers; the birds, our cousins. We end our prayers with the words *all my relations*—and that includes everything that grows, crawls, runs, creeps, hops, and flies."

11

THE SPIRITUAL POWER OF
PLACE

Flashing lightning from its eyes and booming thunder with each flap of its wings, the great Thunderbird, *Wakinyan*, brought down violent storms, moving even the boldest men to pray. The Lakota Sioux elders warned youngsters who went up the mountain in search of inspiration not to go too near the craggy summit: "That is the Wakinyan's place. Do not trespass on it."

The ties that bind Native Americans to their homelands and sacred places are far more complex than mere territorial claims. Deserts, coastlines, mountains, and forests are held sacred, and veneration of the land is inextricably entwined with a tribe's way of life. Indeed, according to Indian tradition, everything on earth—from sand and rock to animals and plants to lightning and thunder—is hallowed. Disturbing or failing to honor any part of it is believed to result in tragic

Above: *Pacific Northwest Clayoquot dance robe*

Left: *Sunlit fog among redwoods*

disharmony. The Indians believe that their physical and mystical connections to their lands are vital not only to the maintenance of their religious practices but also to their very cultural integrity.

In these sacred places, many of which are imbued with healing powers, gods abide, supernatural spirits dwell, and vision quests are made. According to legend, these are the loci of creation—points where the first people of a tribe emerged onto earth—and for many, these are the center of the universe, sacred and holy, where the spiritual powers of place bring transformation, harmony, and rebirth.

Spirits and the Creation Myths

The Algonquian of northern New England call themselves *Wabanaki*, or the original People of Dawnland. As their legend has it, mythic hero Gluskab, a giant, came from across the sea in a granite canoe. When he reached land and found no people to greet him, he drew his great bow and split open an ash tree. When the first humans stepped from the bark, Gluskab did all he could to make their world a more inviting place. He freed the streams and rivers by slaying a froglike monster who was hoarding the waters in its swollen belly. He captured the mighty Wind Eagle but bound it so tightly that a stifling calm descended. Recognizing his error, Gluskab loosened the Wind Eagle's wings, and cool breezes wafted across the land. Gluskab filled the forest with animals to give people plenty to eat. At first, he made the animals too big and they were a threat to the people so he made the animals smaller, and thereafter, when creatures of the forest saw man approaching, they turned and ran. Gluskab taught the people how to track and snare those skittish animals and where to find wild vegetables and herbs for food and medicine. He showed them how to build houses and canoes and kindle fires, and he taught them the names of all the stars that blazed in the heavens. After he had made the world fit for humans, Gluskab left them and went to dwell in the depths of the forest.

The Hualapai came into being in the canyons of the Colorado when the Great Spirit conceived a plan

14

to transform the tall canes that grew by the riverbank into the first humans. Working with the trickster and wonder-worker Coyote, he planned the creation of a vast population. But an errant howl by Coyote pierced the darkness of the land and so angered the Great Spirit that he changed only a few of the stalks into people, and thus the Hualapai remained a sparse tribe which moved back and forth between their low-lying plots and their hunting grounds on the high plateau.

To the south of the Hualapai, life originated for the Upland Yuman, or Yavapai, in the Red Rock Mountains of Sedona. There, in a cliffside cave, Yavapai legends attest that First Woman was embraced by Sun and Cloud and gave birth to the human race. Most of her descendants dispersed, but the Yavapai remained at the center of the world, drawing inspiration from the cave where members of the tribe still pray for friends in need.

The earliest people of the Navajo, or Diné, were First Man and First Woman, who lived near Huerfano Mountain in the Diné Tah. Their initial task was to bring light to the universe. From a large turquoise disk, the couple created the sun and then sculpted the moon from a piece of rock crystal. As darkness gave way to the first dawn, a baby was born on Gobernador Knob. First Man and First Woman found the infant, nestled in a cradleboard of rainbows and sunrays. With help from the spirits—known among the Navajo as Holy People— the couple raised the child on pollen and dew. She grew up to be Changing Woman, the most beautiful maiden who ever lived. It was she who created the Navajo people from sacred cornmeal and scrapings from her own skin. Changing Woman also bore two sons, Monster Slayer and Child Born of Water. In ancient times, these heroes roamed the earth ridding it of monsters and making it safe for humans and animals. Only then, according to the Navajo legend, did the creatures of the earth dwell in peace and harmony.

The Native American peoples of the Northwest Coast trace their origins to the margins of the sea. According to a legend handed down by the Haida, who settled west of the Tsimshian on the Queen Charlotte Islands (Haida Gwaii), the first of their ancestors were coaxed into the world on a desolate beach by Raven him-

15

This fifty-inch birch-bark model canoe is inscribed with a variety of animals. Animals played an important part in Algonquian creation stories.

self—the fabled bird, bringer of light to the world—who was prowling the shore when he came upon a partially open clamshell. Raven was all alone in the world at the time, and eager for company. Bending down to examine the clamshell, he noticed a small face peering timidly out at him. "Come out! Come out!" Raven called and several more small faces soon peeked out from the edge of the shell. Slowly, shyly, the tiny people pushed open the clamshell and climbed out onto the sandy shore. These were the original Haida—the People, as they called themselves—and they emerged from the same watery element that would sustain their descendants.

Further inland, the Mesquakie believe the spirits of their ancestors dwell within the trees of their Iowa homeland. "The murmur of the trees when the wind passes through is but the voices of our grandparents," explained one Mesquakie. The tribe, also known as the Fox Indians, thus considers wood and all objects made from wood to be sacred.

The spiritual power of place speaks to all Native Americans. And whether the spirit is Mother Earth, Father Sky, or the plants, animals, or insects that are sheltered therein, each has a voice.

16

CLOSE TO THE DAWNLAND

For the Algonquian, the rising of the sun from the eastern waters over forests and mountains was a daily reminder of their wondrous emergence as the Original People of Dawnland. The Tsimshian related a story that honored the raven for bringing light from heaven to illuminate the world below. Other tribes told of the Great Hare who sprang from the land of the rising sun and formed a bountiful world for people to inhabit. Both inland and coastal tribes celebrated and gave thanks to the Dawnland, the bright beginning of all things.

Lakeside dawning brings a new day

18

THE GREAT MOUNTAIN
Mount Katahdin in northern Maine

T*he towering grandeur of Mount Katahdin in northern Maine is reflected in the glistening surface of a nearby lake. The peak remains sacred to the Penobscot Indians and other Eastern Abenaki of the area, who refer to it as the Great Mountain and believe that its spirit controls the weather.*

19

LAKE OF THE TRANSFORMER
Lake Champlain

20

The serene expanse of Lake Champlain forms the border between New York and Vermont. According to a legend of the Western Abenaki, the transformer Odzihoso molded himself from mere dust and set about shaping the earth to his liking. When his task was completed, he changed himself into an outcropping of rock in Lake Champlain so that he could forever overlook and admire his handiwork.

21

22

THE GIANT'S CLIFFS
Gay Head on the island of Martha's Vineyard

W*aves roll in from the Atlantic below the clay cliffs of Gay Head on the island of Martha's Vineyard, home to the Wampanoag who migrated from the Massachusetts mainland. Wampanoag lore tells of a protective giant know as Maushop, sent here by the Creator to watch over the people. When the time came for the giant to depart, Wampanoag gathered at the cliffs and watched Maushop swim away in the guise of an immense whale.*

23

24

THE RIVERINE REALM
OF THE LENAPE
Upper Delaware River near Minisink Island

Water cascades *through lush greenery on a tributary of the upper Delaware River, homeland of the Munsee branch of the Lenape, known to European colonists as the Delaware Indians. In early times, the Lenape gathered annually for religious ceremonies on nearby Minisink Island.*

25

26

POWHATAN'S LUSH DOMAIN
The Pamunkey River

T

he Pamunkey River flows past the Pamunkey Indian Reservation, located near land sacred to the followers of Powhatan, whose multitribal chiefdom covered much of Tidewater Virginia in the early 1600s. The leading Powhatan temple was located nearby, and according to tribal tradition, the chief himself was laid to rest in the area.

27

A GIFT FROM THE SKY CHIEF

"Before there were people on the earth," begins a legend handed down by northern California's Modoc people, "the Chief of the Sky Spirits grew tired of his home in the Above World because the air was always brittle with an icy cold. So he carved a hole in the sky with a stone and pushed all the snow and ice down below until he made a great mound that reached from the earth almost to the sky. Today it is known as Mount Shasta."

Pleased with his accomplishment, the Sky Chief stepped from the clouds to Shasta's snowy peak and strode down its slope: "When he was about halfway to the valley below, he began to put his finger to the ground, here and there, here and there. Wherever his finger touched, a tree grew. The snow melted in his footsteps, and the water ran down in rivers."

As this tale illustrates, the Modoc, like other Indians, recognized the handiwork of higher powers everywhere they looked—in sculpted peaks and sunlit valleys, in murmuring rivers and silent glades. Their homeland was a fresh and vibrant place, where the potent beings that shaped the earth still touched and inspired the people.

To the native peoples, the lush rain forest, the marshlands, the wooded foothills and mountains, the shimmering beaches, and the blazing deserts all made demands and bestowed rewards, fostering a unique way of life.

What the occupants of these diverse locales held in common were the beliefs that every life-sustaining creature and element came to them as a gift from the spirit world, and that nothing in their environment should be taken for granted. As a Yuki holy man of the Mendocino woodlands explained as he led initiates around the rim of their tribal domain, "The rock did not come here by itself. This tree does not stand here of itself. There is One who made all this, who shows us everything."

29

Mount Shasta

THIS HALLOWED TERRAIN

Certain spectacular sites, such as those shown on the following pages, have long been regarded as especially holy by the desert Indians. Some of these landmarks are honored as the abodes of gods or supernatural spirits. Others are revered as sites of creation, where tribal ancestors came into being. Ancestral legends imbue some landscapes with healing powers. And sacred places are frequently sources of water—the literal life-giver in the arid world of the desert.

Left: *Sunset on Shiprock, New Mexico*

MOUNTAIN SPIRIT
San Francisco Peaks

Looming over the valley below and the desert beyond, Arizona's snow-clad San Francisco Peaks inspire reverence in several tribes. The Hopi believe that the cloud-swathed range shelters the essential rain spirits. For the Navajo, the peaks mark one of the four corners of their ancestral lands. And the San Carlos Apache say beneficent beings, called the Mountain Spirit People, dwell atop the peaks.

32

33

CENTER OF THE UNIVERSE
Baboquivari Peak, Arizona

The evening sun casts its radiance on Baboquivari Peak in south-central Arizona, venerated by Papago (Tohono O'odham) and Pima Indians as the physical and spiritual center of their universe. Papago legend attests that the stunning sunsets were a gift from their creator, Elder Brother, the spirit of goodness, who watches over the people from his home on the stony slope.

34

THE HEALING SPRING
Havasu Canyon

An oasis in the
*midst of the sunbaked Grand Canyon, Havasu
Canyon has been inhabited and honored by the
Havasupai Indians for countless centuries. The
Havasupai, whose name translates as "people
of the blue-green water," believe the springs
that feed the canyon's creeks and falls possess
curative powers.*

36

38

THE PORTAL OF LIFE
Spirit Mountain

*C*rowned by
white granite bluffs, Spirit Mountain in south-
ern Nevada is holy to the Mohave and the
Hualapai, as well as to all other Indian peoples
whose language traces to the Yuman tongue.
These so-called Yuman tribes regard the rugged
peak as the portal through which human life
emerged after the world had been ravaged by
a great flood.

39

40

SPIDER WOMAN
Canyon de Chelly

A sandstone spire jutting 800 feet above the floor of Arizona's Canyon de Chelly, Spider Rock—the formation at near left—is honored by the Hopi and Navajo as the lair of the earth goddess Spider Woman. According to Hopi legend, Spider Woman serves as a powerful link between the human world and the world of the divine. The Navajo invoke her name to discipline unruly children.

41

KATZIMO
The Enchanted Mesa

Rising like an island from the sandy bottom of the New Mexican desert, Katzimo, or Enchanted Mesa, has long been revered by the Acoma Indians as the site of their ancestral pueblo. According to legend, most of the tribe was tending crops in the valley below when a savage storm swept away the stone steps to the 400-foot mesa, stranding a few doomed souls at its top and forcing the tribe's relocation.

42

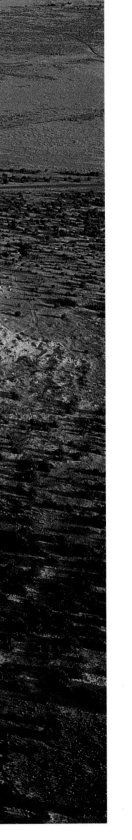

44

MOUNTAIN SPIRIT DANCERS
Guadalupe Peak

From caves high atop *Texas's Guadalupe Peak—the summit at far left—the first mountain spirit dancers entered the world, according to the Mescalero Apache. Considered a conduit to heavenly power, the beings are impersonated by masked performers in the Mountain Spirit Dance, an age-old Apache ritual used to cure illness, banish bad fortune, and usher a girl into maturity.*

45

LONG SASH AND HIS PEOPLE

The bright star that rises in the east soon after autumn sunset is Long Sash, who guided the ancestors of the Pueblo from the north to their present home. He was a famous warrior, and the people followed him because they knew he could lead them in defense against their enemies. Someone was always attacking the villages and wrecking the fields. The enemies captured women and children for slaves and killed many of the men, until Long Sash came to the rescue.

"Take us away from here," the people begged him. "Lead us to a new land, where we can live peacefully."

"My children," Long Sash said, "are you sure you want to leave? Life is hard here, I know, but it will not be easy anywhere. There will be dangers on the way if you travel. Some will be sick; many will be hungry and thirsty; perhaps some of you may die. Think, and be sure you want to take that risk."

"We will face any hardships," the people promised him. "Only lead us away from this dark country, to a place where we may have light and life of our own."

So Long Sash started out, and the people followed him. They set their feet on the Endless Trail that stretches like a white band across the sky. This was the road they were going to follow until they found a place of their own.

As the people traveled along the Endless Trail with Long Sash, they began to grow tired and discouraged. Some of them quarreled with one another. They had little clothing and less food. Long Sash had to teach his followers how to hunt for food and how to make clothing from feathers. At last he led them to a country that was so new that even Long Sash had never been there before.

In this new country there was no darkness, it was daylight all the time. The people walked and walked, and when they were too tired to go on they rested. Children were born and old people died and still they journeyed.

The quarrels grew more bitter, and the people began to fight among themselves, exchanging blows and inflicting wounds. At last Long Sash said to them, "This must stop. You are hurting yourselves worse than your

Wave cloud in an autumn sunset

enemies hurt you. If you are to come to the place of your own, there can never be violence among you. Now you must decide. We will stop here and rest. Many of the women are ready to have their babies. We will wait until the children are delivered and the mothers are strong. Then you must make your own decision, whether you will follow me or take another trail."

There where the two very bright stars are north of Long Sash in the sky, the people rested and made up their minds. Those two bright stars became known as the Place of Decision, and people look up to them for help today, when they come to the turning points in their lives. We all have decisions to make as long as we are on the earth: good or bad, forward or backward, kind or unkind. Those stars can tell us what to do.

When the people had rested and felt stronger, they were ready to go ahead with Long Sash. They told him so, and everybody went forward again. Long Sash watched, to be sure that his children traveled with good hearts and love toward each other.

But Long Sash himself was growing tired, and his own heart was empty and doubting. He heard strange voices speaking in his mind, and could not tell who spoke, or what they were trying to say to him. At last he decided to answer the voices. As he spoke to the unseens, his own people gathered around him to listen.

"Show me a sign to tell me who you are, fathers and mothers," Long Sash began. "My people are tired and I am growing old. Give me a word to tell me we are on the right path and will soon reach our home."

Then while his people watched him, frightened, Long Sash appeared to go to sleep. He dropped down where he had been sitting and his eyes were closed. He lay without moving while the people stayed beside him, because they did not know what to do. They grew more and more afraid.

At last Long Sash opened his eyes. He looked at the people who had gathered around him while he slept. "Don't be frightened," Long Sash told them. "I have been given many signs and promises. The worst part of your journey is over, and we will soon reach its end."

"That's good. Thank you," all the people said.

"Many people will reach this Place of Doubt in their lives," Long Sash went on. "When that happens, you should pray to the Above Persons, your fathers and mothers, for help and for guidance. In order to remind you of that, I will leave my headdress here, where people can look up and see it."

He laid his headdress down, and it became a bright, comforting cluster of stars. And so the people went

48

on traveling, and the story of their journey is told in the stars above. Where there are three bright stars close together, they represent two young men who made a drag and fastened their load on it. Then, because there were two of them, they could add an old woman's load and go on, pulling three loads on the drag. Those stars are a reminder of the helpfulness of the young men, and of their thoughtfulness of other people.

At last the people came to the end of their journey, and to the Middle Place which was to be their home forever.

TEWA

MY BREATH BECAME

The day broke with slender rain
The place which is called "lightning's water stands,"
The place which is called "where dawn strikes,"
Four places where it is called "it dawns with life,"
I land there.
The sky boys, I go among them.
He came to me with long life.
When he talked over my body with the longest life,
The voice of the thunder spoke well four times,
He spoke four times to me with life.
Holy sky youth spoke to me four times.
When he talked to me my breath became.

APACHE

49

Apache dancer with gaan mask

THE SACRED HILLS

Described as the "heart of everything that is," the Black Hills straddling the border of South Dakota and Wyoming have long held great spiritual significance for the native peoples of the region. Among the world's oldest mountain ranges, their dark, pine-forested bluffs rise from the surrounding prairie like mysterious islands in an ocean of grass. For centuries, Indians have climbed the craggy hills at left to commune with their spirits and seek guidance from visions. Indeed, for tribes of the area, the Black Hills remain the holiest of places, a wilderness shrine suffused with both physical beauty and supernatural power.

The legends associated with the Black Hills and nearby features, such as the Badlands, express the conviction of Native Americans that the land has shaped their destiny. Both the Cheyenne and the Lakota Sioux say the region was once the site of a great and fateful contest. According to a legend of the Lakota, at one time there were no Black Hills interrupting the endless stretch of plains, and humans and their fellow creatures preyed indiscriminately upon one another. To bring order to this chaotic world, man summoned all the animals to a race. Following an enormous circular path outlined on the prairie, the creatures raced around and around in a mad frenzy. The tumult seemed to disturb the spirits, for soon the path sank beneath the racers' pounding feet, and the ground within the circle rose up, forming a mountainous bulge that eventually burst and showered the creatures with debris. Many were killed, including the monsters called the Unktehi, whose huge bones can still be found in the area. Humans survived the holocaust and claimed the right to prey on other animals. But the Black Hills standing at the site of the ancient cataclysm serve as a reminder to the people that their strength is insignificant compared with the awesome power of the spirits abiding in the earth.

51

Left: *Rainbow over the Badlands in the Black Hills of South Dakota*

PEAK OF LEGEND
Chief Mountain, Montana

Sacred to the Blackfeet, Blood, and Piegan Indians, Montana's Chief Mountain soars 9,080 feet above sea level, making it visible anywhere in Blackfeet territory. According to Blackfeet legend, the mountain was the only land left unsubmerged after a great flood covered the earth. From that spot, the Creator, Old Man, made the present earth.

52

53

54

WHERE GIANTS STRUGGLED
Bear Butte, South Dakota

Protruding from the plains just east of the Black Hills proper is a lonely and majestic outcropping, dubbed Bear Butte by the Lakota. According to tribal legend, the butte was formed in ancient times as the result of a titanic struggle between a huge bear and a monstrous Unktehi. For days, the two giants clashed, shedding blood in streams, until at last the bear conceded defeat and went off on its own to die. When the bear collapsed, the earth convulsed and covered its body. All that remained was the massive mound. Atop this butte, the Lakota believe their chief, Crazy Horse, received supernatural powers from the spirit of a bear. The Cheyenne, for their part, consider Bear Butte the most sacred place on earth. It was there that the Cheyenne prophet Sweet Medicine received the four Sacred Arrows that brought blessings to his people. To this day, the Cheyenne and Lakota make pilgrimages to Bear Butte to pray and fast.

55

56

PLACE OF THE THUNDERBIRD
Harney Peak, South Dakota

The granite summit of Harney Peak, highest of the Black Hills, was said to be the nesting place of a legendary creature long dreaded and revered by the Lakota—the frightful Wakinyan, or "Thunderbird." This fantastic beast of Indian lore was a guardian of truth, killing liars with lightning bolts from its beak and eyes.

57

58

CREATURE OF THE LAKOTA
Devils Tower

Looming above the Belle Fourche River in northeastern Wyoming, the great shaft of stone known as Devils Tower has long been associated by Plains Indians with the creature the Lakota call Mató, or the "Bear." According to the Kiowa, a spirit once appeared to a proud young girl in the form of a great bear and changed her into that same shape. Reveling in her newfound power, the giant bear girl chased after her seven siblings and threatened to devour them, until they jumped atop a low rock and prayed for help to the Great Spirit. At once the rock began to grow upward, elevating them beyond their sister's reach. Enraged, she leapt and clawed at the sides of the rock. But her siblings grew ever more distant, rising clear into the heavens, where they became the seven stars of the Pleiades. Left behind on the tower's walls were signs of the bear girl's thwarted fury—long claw marks engraved deep in the stone.

59

FROM THE PRIMORDIAL WATERS
Badlands, South Dakota

Sculpted by countless centuries of erosion into a haunting landscape of hills, canyons, and gullies, the desert region stretching east of the Black Hills is known to the Lakota as Makoshicha, or the "Badlands." Once covered by an inland sea, and later roamed by dinosaurs, the Badlands and its fossil remains are associated in Lakota lore with the Unktehi, monsters inhabiting the primordial waters from which the earth emerged. According to one Lakota legend, long ago the Unktehi turned against the human race and began causing devastating floods, thus angering the Wakinyan, who worried that there would be no people left to pray to the Thunderbird and dream of its power. The Wakinyan sent down blazing thunderbolts that dried up the floodwaters and consumed the malicious Unktehi, whose bones still lie amid the tortuous Badlands to remind people of the terror and wonder of the spirits.

60

61

EMERGENCE SONG

Together we emerge with our rattles;

Together we emerge with our rattles,

Bright-hued feathers in our headdresses.

With our nyñnyirsa we went down;

With our nyñnyirsa we went down,

Wearing Yoku feathers in our headdresses.

This is the White Land; we arrive singing,

Headdresses waving in the breeze.

We have come! We have come!

The land trembles with our dancing and singing.

On these black mountains all are singing,

Headdresses waving, headdresses waving.

We all rejoice! We all rejoice!

Singing, dancing, the mountains trembling.

PIMA

Above: *Summoning the Spirit*

Left: *Nez Percé costumed in a feathered headdress and bustle*

FACING A SPIRITUAL
QUEST

The vision quest—individual religious revelations through dreams and visions—has long been the focal point of the spiritual life of most Native Americans. Visions provide access to power, the current of supernatural force that courses beneath the surface of every aspect of Indian life. The Abenaki have a saying: "The Great Spirit is in all things; he is in the air we breathe." A Teton Sioux expressed the same thought in a different way: "It is the general belief of the Indians that after a man dies, his spirit is somewhere on the earth or in the sky, we do not know exactly where, but we believe that his spirit still lives. So it is with Wakan Tanka. We believe that he is everywhere, yet he is to us as the spirits of our friends whose voices we cannot hear."

Even so, some places and objects are more highly charged with power than

Above: A petroglyph painting probably representing the guardian spirit of the quester

Left: The Grand Teton Mountains, a range considered so sacred and powerful by the Shoshone Indians that one shouldn't even point at them

others. Although all power springs from the Great Spirit, it manifests itself in different ways; from great elemental forces like the sun, the moon, and the winds to individual rocks, animals, and trees. Mountaintops and places near water are also full of power. Conversely, other spots are especially dangerous—particularly grave sites, where malevolent spirits of the dead may lurk. If the spirits are not appeased by correct behavior, their power can cause harm.

A solitary vision quest, however, is by no means the only route to power. Indians also seek visions through participation in group ceremonies such as the Sun Dance, the great summer ritual of the Plains Indians. And sometimes the visions come unbidden, through the medium of dreams. Several Indian communities put particular emphasis on this channel to the supernatural, among them the Mohave, who live in Arizona and California, and the Iroquois of New York State, of whom a Jesuit missionary noted 300 years ago: "They consider the dream as the master of their lives. It is the God of the country. It is this that dictates to them their feasts, their hunting, their fishing, their wars, their trade with the French, their remedies, their dances, their games, their songs."

66

Women could dream themselves power, which could be used in such traditionally female fields as treating sick children, preparing food, or gathering plants. As a rule, however, strong taboos kept them from participating in male activities. A woman's unique power of giving life was considered antithetic to a man's power to hunt and kill. Traditionally, girls were sequestered in small huts at the time of their first menstruation, typically for a period of four to ten days—a rite that paralleled the adolescent male's vision quest.

For boys, however, preparations for the vision quest often began well before puberty. In some communities, children as young as seven or eight were denied food for a day to accustom them to fasting; as they grew older, they would train themselves to endure longer periods. In the meantime, their fathers and grandfathers talked to them about visions to prepare them for the experience. In doing so, the boys learned ancestral lore, with the result that members of each Indian community have tended to experience similar visions.

THE DREAM SEEKERS

Native Americans have tradition-
ally viewed success in life as a gift from the gods. Seeking this gift, countless
Indians have undertaken solitary journeys to remote locations in the mountains or forests, where they fast and pray in the hope of receiving spiritual
guidance in a powerful dream. Among several tribes, these vision quests
marked the passage into adulthood for adolescent boys. In some communities, the practice endures today.

Although details of the ordeal vary from tribe to tribe, most vision
quests lasted between four and six days. After a ritual purification, some Sioux
questers spent the entire period in an earthen pit, naked except for a buffalo
robe. Crow youths often slept inside a symbolic fasting bed, a stone enclosure
facing east so that "the blessings of the morning sun may enter directly" upon
them. Among the Indians of the Pacific Northwest, repeated bathing in frigid
pools was the route to spiritual revelation. The Luiseno of southern California
used the hallucinogenic jimson weed to induce a vision.

When a vision did come—usually in the form of an animal, an insect,
a natural phenomenon, or some legendary creature—it revealed the dreamer's
guardian for life. Many tribes have encouraged their adult members to continue
seeking visions as a form of spiritual renewal. As one experienced dreamer once
explained, it was only during a dream that "you see something with your inner
eyes, with all your soul and spirit."

The Mesquakie believed that a hawk's feather, such as the one on this scalp-lock ornament, gave a youth courage

"After going so many
suns without food,
I was sleeping.
It was just like
dreaming,
what I saw.
A form stood in the
air fronting me.
It was the spirit of
a wolf that
appeared to me.
Yellowlike in color,
it sort of floated
in the air.
Like a human being
it talked to me, and
gave me its power."

—*YELLOW WOLF*
NEZ PERCÉ

NEZ PERCÉ SEEKERS

Wallowa Mountains in northeastern Oregon

A*Native*
American tipi sits on a ridge at the base of the
Wallowa Mountains in northeastern Oregon.
When the Nez Percé Indians occupied this
region, the range was one of their most popular
vision quest sites.

69

A swan's-head
medicine object honors
a Nez Percé guardian
spirit. After a creature
appeared to an Indian in a vision, he would
commonly kill one of its species and keep part
of the dead animal as a charm.

SEEKING A VISION
Rocky Mountains, northwestern Montana

Generations of Blackfeet youth have fasted and sought visions in the aspen forests of the Rocky Mountains of northwestern Montana.

70

The design for this 1930s deer-hide tunic first appeared to Big Plume, a nineteenth-century Blackfeet warrior, in an adolescent vision quest. The rights to the design were passed down through ensuing generations.

"When my eldest son
died, I felt his loss so
deeply that I climbed
to the mountain's
summit and lay there
fasting for ten days
and ten nights. During
that time, the spirit of
the mountain appeared
and gave me a
medicine robe. He
instructed me how to
make the robe and
said that if I used it in
doctoring I would be
endowed with wisdom
and power."

—BRINGS DOWN THE SUN
BLACKFEET

71

"A bear lifted me up so that I could see all the earth. He made me touch his teeth; he had none at all. 'You may jump among high cliffs or do what you please,' said he. 'You cannot die. When you have no more teeth and all your hair is white, you shall fall asleep without awaking.'"

—*FULL MOUTH BUFFALO, CROW*

72

SANCTUARIES
Foothills of the Rocky Mountains

The eastern slopes of the Rocky Mountains in Montana have long provided sanctuaries for Crow vision seekers.

Crow warriors often recorded their visions on shield covers like the one below. Since the Crow believed that revealing a dream robs it of its potency, the meaning of this design is unknown. The weasel pelt underneath is a medicine bundle imbued with exceptional power; its owner created it after a weasel appeared to him in a vision.

73

JOURNEY INTO MANHOOD
Great Lakes

Among the Menominee of the western Great Lakes region, boys blackened their faces with charcoal and pushed deep into woods like those shown here to seek a vision. Although the vision quest was optional among some tribes, for the Menominee, it was a crucial part of a boy's journey toward manhood.

This Menominee medicine bag was fashioned from beaver skin and embroidered with porcupine quills. Inside was a variety of sacred objects related to the owner's vision and used by him to seek protection and guidance from his guardian spirit.

74

"After I had fasted eight days, a tall man with a big red mouth appeared from the east. The solid earth bent under his steps as though it was a marsh. He said, 'I have pity on you. You shall live to see your own gray hairs and those of your children. You shall never be in danger if you make your-self a war club such as I have and always carry it with you wherever you go.'"

—MENOMINEE ELDER

75

PLACE OF VISIONS
Pictured Rocks National Lakeshore, Ontario

O*n the north shore of Lake Superior, waves pound shore rocks and cliffs that provided Ojibwa vision seekers the solitude necessary for communing with the spirit world. The region is covered with pictographs drawn by young men who wished to record their visions.*

Before embarking on a vision quest, an Ojibwa commonly filled a pouch like the one below with an offering of tobacco. Although such bags were usually decorated with the image of their most powerful sky deity, Thunderbird, the quill work design on this one most likely depicts a horse.

76

"The loon flew out
into the lake and
brought me a fish to
eat and told me that
I would have good
luck in hunting and
fishing; that I would
live to a good old
age; and that I
would never be
wounded by a shot-
gun or rifle. This bird
who had blessed me
was the kind that one
rarely has a chance
of shooting. From
that time on the loon
was my guardian
spirit."

*—ANONYMOUS OJIBWA FROM
SAMIA, ONTARIO*

77

CHRONICLES OF A PEOPLE

Symbols, inscribed by Indians on stone, bark, hide, or other materials, brought events or concepts to mind in a way that surpassed words, for the pictographs conveyed profound beliefs and perceptions with a visionary clarity. Lame Deer, a Lakota Sioux holy man, explained the power of the pictographs in this way: "We see in the world around us many symbols that teach us the meaning of life. . . . To you symbols are just words, spoken or written in a book. To us they are part of nature, part of ourselves—the earth, the sun, the wind, and the rain."

Ritual objects are often inscribed with symbolic markings representing powerful and sacred spirits. The concentric circles drawn on shields, drums, and even painted on the bodies of the Plains Indian warriors symbolize their belief that all things in the universe are interconnected in a divine and harmonious fashion—that the power of the world works in circles.

Fertility images on a Zuni prayer bowl

"A people without history is like wind on the buffalo grass." That Sioux saying expresses the universal determination of tribal peoples to preserve a record of their past. Indians have been recording their traditions pictorially for thousands of years. The first Americans may well have portrayed the animals on which they depended for survival as a way of appealing to those creatures spiritually and ensuring a bountiful hunt. Indian artists, in recent times, continue to depict the close bonds between humans and animals.

For Indian chroniclers, inscription was as important as battles or peace councils. Renderings of rituals, ceremonies, and legends were all part of a tribe's sacred history. Lacking written languages, native chroniclers of the Plains used pictographs to denote a significant event for each year on their winter counts—so-called because the keeper of the count added a new symbol to the hide every winter to represent the preceding year. Those revealing calendars, supplemented by the stories told by elders, helped youngsters learn the lessons of history by envisioning the experiences of earlier generations.

78

Pictographs on a canyon wall in Canyonlands, Utah

A Legacy Inscribed

Inspired by unknown impulses, Indians of North America have left various designs on the canyons, cliffs, and boulders of their native landscapes. Many of these pictures, incised or painted, have survived to the present day. The mysterious rock art drawings include ghostly human forms, game animals, abstractions with spirals, and meandering lines. They might have been designed to propitiate supernatural forces and ensure a group's general prosperity. Works depicting masked figures, elaborate headdresses, and richly decorated clothing are probably related to ceremonies conducted by shamans. And various geometric signs have been linked to recordkeeping or to the marking of cyclical natural events, such as the summer solstice.

Above: *A quartzite buffalo effigy of the northern Plains people found in Alberta, Canada*
Left: *Newspaper Rock, petroglyph in the mountains of Petrified Forest National Park, Arizona*

PAINTED SYMBOLS

*L*ewis and Clark shipped this buffalo hide, depicting a battle between the Mandan and their Sioux rivals, from Fort Mandan to President Jefferson in early 1805.

Warriors in action on this late 1800s muslin dress of Sioux design exemplify the vivid chronicling typical of the Plains dwellers' possessions.

82

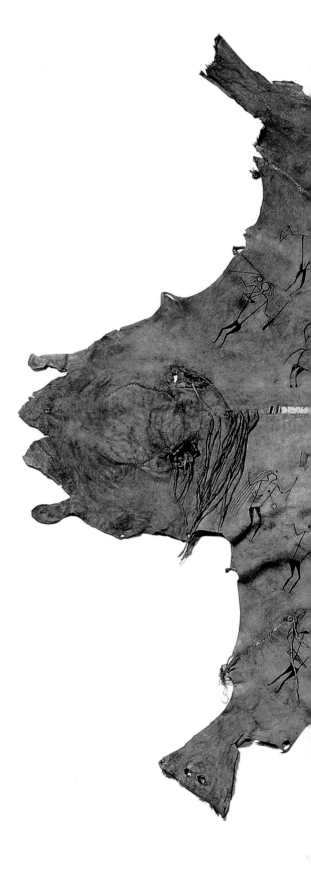

HOLY GHOST
Maze District, Canyonlands

Tapering mummy-like forms cover part of a 140-foot-long canyon wall in Utah known as the Great Gallery. Possibly 2,000 years old, this mural is one of the largest surviving examples of rock art in North America. The figures found in rock art range from simple faces with no outline to complex depictions of warriors and spirit guardian figures. The Indians may also have depicted animals as a means of increasing the game supply, or of recording a tally of animals.

84

Hunting Panel, Nine Mile Canyon, Utah

CRYING FOR A VISION

One morning, an hour or so after dawn, a young Oglala Sioux climbed purposefully through the fir trees that carpet the Black Hills of South Dakota. A buffalo robe was draped over one arm, and he held a pipe in front of him. Its bowl was sealed with tallow so that it could not be smoked. The youth walked with the resolute step of one who knew exactly where he had to go and what he had to do. He had set off on the age-old quest known to his people as *hanbleceya*, or crying for a vision—an ordeal performed by most Sioux males as a means of establishing personal contact with *Wakan Tanka*, or Great Mystery.

Helpers had gone before him, and when the young Indian arrived at his hilltop destination he found that they had prepared the site carefully. Five wooden poles had been planted in the ground. The outer shafts, aligned with the four cardinal points of the compass, stood about ten paces from a center post that symbolized the upper and lower worlds of the Sioux universe. A bundle of sacred objects, wrapped in hide, adorned each pole, and a pinch of *kinnikinnick*, a powerful mixture of tobacco, various grasses, bearberries, and shavings from the inner bark of trees, had been placed beneath the center pole. The bed of sage that they had laid on the ground for him to rest on stretched eastward from the center pole, so that when the youth awoke in the morning he would be facing the rising sun. After completing their work, the assistants had ridden back to the village. The young man was alone with the woods and the sky.

In accordance with ancient ritual, the youth went directly to the center pole, then turned westward to look at the rolling hills. Holding the pipe in both hands, he cried out to Wakan Tanka to take pity on him that his people might live. Over the hours that followed, the vision seeker repeated the cry many times, both aloud and silently, as he walked in an exceedingly slow and respectful manner between the poles, delivering his prayer first to the west, then to the north, the east, and the south, returning each time to the center post. After a few rounds, he raised his pipe in supplication to the sky. Pointing the pipe to the ground, he begged assistance from the earth.

Throughout the day, the youth kept careful watch over every living thing that shared the solitude of his aerie. He knew that Wakan Tanka usually manifested itself in the form of animals or birds. Well after the last

86

light had drained away behind the hills, the young man continued to pace between the poles, repeating his plea to the starlit sky. Even when fatigue finally overcame him and he lay down to rest on his scented bed of sage, he did not give up the quest, for he knew that the most powerful visions often come in dreams. He arose from time to time during the night to resume his prayers, and by daybreak he was up again, raising his pipe in silent offering to the morning star. The ordeal extended through another day and night.

At the end of the appointed time, the helpers returned to carry the young man back to camp. Although the helpers burned with curiosity, they refrained from questioning him, and the young man kept his silence. Back in the village, he was ushered into the presence of the holy man to whom he had made his vow.

"You have now sent a voice with your pipe to Wakan Tanka," the holy man said. "That pipe is now very sacred, for the whole universe has seen it. And since you are about to put this pipe to your mouth, you should tell us nothing but the truth. The pipe is Wakan and knows all things; you cannot fool it."

The holy man removed the tallow, filled the bowl with kinnikinnick, and lighted it with a coal from the fire. After the pipe had been offered to the powers of the six directions of the universe and passed around the circle of listeners four times, the quester began his report. Several eagles had flown near him, he said, but said nothing. A red-breasted woodpecker, however, had alighted on one of the offering poles, and he had heard the bird say faintly yet distinctly: "Be attentive and have no fear; but pay no attention to any bad thing that may come and talk to you." Later on, he saw the morning star change color, from red to blue to yellow to white. Then, just before the end of his vigil, the woodpecker returned and spoke clearly to him: "Friend, be attentive as you walk."

After the youth had completed his report, the holy man passed him the pipe to smoke and then summed up the lessons that could be drawn from the quest. The four colors of the morning star, he explained, represented the four stages of life—infancy, youth, adulthood, and old age—through which all creatures must pass in their journey from birth to death. The message from the woodpecker meant that the young man should always remember Wakan Tanka as he walked the path of life and be attentive to the signs that the Great Mystery had vouchsafed to humanity. Only thus would he grow in wisdom.

The holy man concluded by thanking Wakan Tanka: "You have established a relationship with this young man; and through this relationship he will bring strength to his people and thus we all give thanks to you."

87

THE SHAMAN'S SONG

Even though every shaman possessed a potent set of tools that he employed for healing, nowhere were these sets more elaborate than among the tribes residing in the Pacific Northwest. One particularly powerful Tlingit shaman was discovered buried near Dry Bay, Alaska, along with no fewer than forty-five instruments, including eight masks, four rattles, three batons, three necklaces, and an amulet of spruce root and ermine skins. Each one of these objects had been carved or painted with an assortment of supernatural powers known as *yek*; these were the spirit helpers of the shaman who had appeared to him during his initiatory vision.

So powerful was the shaman's kit that it was never allowed inside a house, except during a curing ceremony. Tradition required that it be stored out-of-doors, often in a hollow tree deep in the forest.

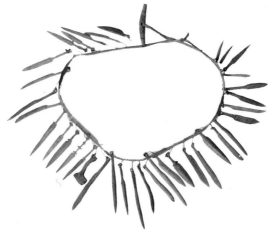

Above: *The tiny horn knives on this Inuit amulet belt were the sole insignia of a Netsilik shaman's rank*
Left: *Ceremonial opening of a Salish tribal council*

Haida shaman's necklace

90

Shaman's baton

A soul-catcher charm

Tlingit moose-hide apron

HAIDA SHAMAN'S CHARMS

This Haida shaman's necklace features charms that rattled as he danced, creating a rhythmic accompaniment to the healing ritual. A soul-catcher charm (lower left) consists of a carved, hollow bone with abalone inset. A host of violent spirits populate a shaman's baton (left), including a land otter crushed beneath a disembodied face and a crow with a naked, wide-eyed human in its beak. The shaman used the staff like a spear or club to combat malicious supernatural enemies. A Tlingit moose-hide apron is painted with figures representing a shaman's spiritual assistants and decorated with ivory and bone charms. The jangling of the charms summoned the spirit helpers to aid in the healing.

92

Shaman's curing drum

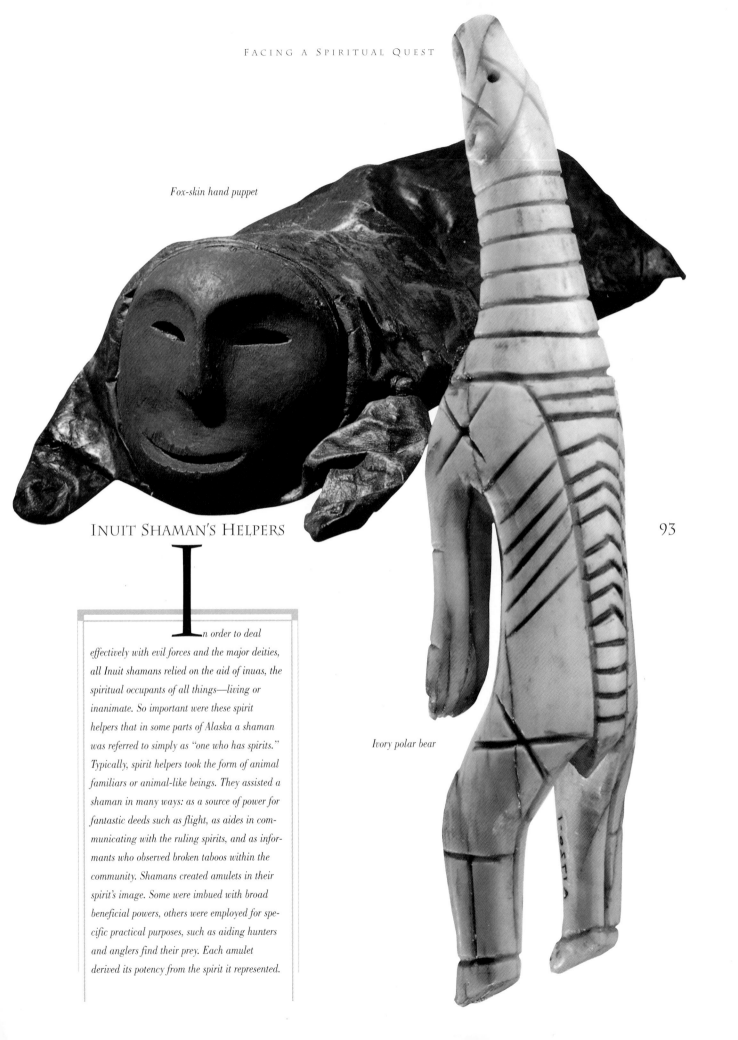

Fox-skin hand puppet

INUIT SHAMAN'S HELPERS

93

In order to deal effectively with evil forces and the major deities, all Inuit shamans relied on the aid of inuas, the spiritual occupants of all things—living or inanimate. So important were these spirit helpers that in some parts of Alaska a shaman was referred to simply as "one who has spirits." Typically, spirit helpers took the form of animal familiars or animal-like beings. They assisted a shaman in many ways: as a source of power for fantastic deeds such as flight, as aides in communicating with the ruling spirits, and as informants who observed broken taboos within the community. Shamans created amulets in their spirit's image. Some were imbued with broad beneficial powers, others were employed for specific practical purposes, such as aiding hunters and anglers find their prey. Each amulet derived its potency from the spirit it represented.

Ivory polar bear

PRAYERS TO THE SPIRITS

According to the Omaha tribe, a child during its infancy had no recognized existence as an individual or distinct member of the tribe, but remained as a part of its parents. When a child could walk alone, he was initiated into the tribal organization through certain religious rites. Only later, after his mind had "become white," as the Indians say, did a child's responsible individual life begin. This expression referred to the dawn, to the passing of night into day, and represented the coming of the child out of the period where nothing was clearly apprehended into a time when it could readily recall past events with distinctive detail. This mastery of the minutiae of passing occurrences indicated that a stage of growth had been reached where the youth could be inducted into the religious mysteries through a distinct personal experience acquired in the rite, Noń-zhiń-zhoń, a rite which brought the youth into what was believed to be direct communication with the supernatural powers.

In preparation for this rite, the Omaha youth was taught the Tribal Prayer. He was to sing it during the four nights and days of his vigil in some lonely place. As he left his home, his parents put clay on his head. To teach him self-control, they placed a bow and arrows in his hand, with the injunction not to use them during his long fast, no matter how great the temptation might be. He was bidden to weep as he sang the prayer, and to wipe his tears with the palms of his hands, to lift his wet hands to heaven, and then lay them on the earth. With these instructions the youth departed, to begin the trial of his endurance. When at last he fell into a sleep or trance, the vision came of bird, beast, or cloud, bringing with it a cadence. This song then became ever after the medium of communication between the man and the mysterious power typified in his vision. All mystery songs—the songs sung when medicine was administered, when a man hunted for game, and when he desired to look into the future or sought supernatural guidance—originated in this manner.

94

THE NIGHT CHANT

In beauty

you shall be my representation

In beauty

you shall be my song

In beauty

you shall be my medicine

In beauty

my holy medicine

NAVAJO

CONCERNING WISDOM

I perform the Beauty Way.

I am over eighty years old.

I have been learning

since I was eleven years old.

I want someone to learn

what I have been learning.

NAVAJO

95

MEDICINE MAN'S PRAYER

Listen, my dream!

This you told me should be done.

This you said should be the way.

You said it would cure the sick.

Help me now.

Do not lie to me.

Help me, Sun person.

Help me to cure this sick man.

BLACKFEET

THE SACRED POWER OF
CEREMONY

For the tribes of the Great Plains, life's path has always traced a circle. As a Cheyenne elder expressed the view of his people: "The beginning and end of life come together in the East. In the beginning of life there is the child's cry, announcing the new life. And in the end there is the old man's prayer." For the neighboring Sioux, every facet of being possesses a circular dimension. Lame Deer, the great-grandson of a Sioux war leader, calls this concept both symbol and reality, expressing the harmony of life. "Our circle is timeless, flowing," he explains. "It is new life emerging from death—life winning out over death." To these warriors and buffalo hunters, the sky, the earth, and the stars were round. The whirling movement of the wind traced multitudinous circles. Always repeating their endless rhythms, the seasons sketch the same

Above: *Buckskin shield is a ritual item worn on the back of one of the Hopi Priests during the Flute Ceremony*
Left: *Sunset over Teton Range and Snake River at Schwabacher Landing, Wyoming*

pattern. Herein lay power. "Everything the power of the world does is done in a circle," the famous Oglala Sioux holy man Black Elk once remarked. "The life of man is a circle from childhood to childhood, and so it is in everything where power moves."

For Native Americans, power meant the spiritual power of the divinities that dwelt everywhere—in the earth and sky, in rocks and rivers, in great herds of buffalo and green stalks of corn. As Indians journeyed along life's earthly trail, they appealed time and again to the spirits for help and guidance. "To us, the spirit world seemed very near, and we did nothing without taking thought of the gods," said a modern Hidatsa, whose ancestors once lived in earthen lodges along the Missouri River in present-day North Dakota. "If we would begin a journey, form a war party, hunt, trap eagles, fish, or plant corn, we first prayed to the spirits."

Only by consulting the spirits at each juncture could an individual's safety and happiness be secured. In various tribes, not only was a child's name consecrated ceremoniously, but a baby's first laugh, first step, or first haircut might also call for sacred rites. At the time of puberty, adolescent boys and girls were initiated into adulthood, often with elaborate ceremony. The middle years brought more rituals, sometimes connected with membership in secret societies, organized for all sorts of community purposes including war, healing, record-keeping, rainmaking, and the dramatization of tribal legends. With death came yet another series of rites, easing the passage of the soul into the spirit world.

98

PRAYER TO A DEAD BUCK

In the future that we may continue to hold each other with the turquoise hand

Now that you may return to the place from which you came

In the future as time goes on that I may rely on you for food

To the home of the dawn you are starting to return

With the jet hoofs you are starting to return

By means of the zigzag lightning you are starting to return

By the evening twilight your legs are yellow

That way you are starting to return

By the white of dawn your buttocks are white and that way you are starting to return

A dark tail is in your tail and that way you are starting to return

A haze is in your fur and that way you are starting to return

A growing vegetation is in your ears and that way you are starting to return

A mixture of beautiful flowers and water is in your intestines and that way you are starting to return

May turquoise be in your liver and abalone shell the partition between your heart and intestines

and that way you are starting to return

May red shell be your lungs and white shell be your windpipe and that way you are starting to return

May dark wind and straight lightning be your speech and that way you are starting to return

There you have returned within the interior of the jet basket in the midst of the beautiful flower pollens

Beautifully you have arrived home

Beautifully may you and I both continue to live

From this day may you lead the other game along the trails, that I may hunt

Because I have obeyed all the restrictions laid down by your god in hunting and skinning you

Therefore I ask for this luck: that I may continue to have good luck in hunting you.

NAVAJO

99

THE VENERABLE POTLATCH

Ancestral connections between families and supernatural beings formed the framework of Native American societies—a framework that was most carefully defined among the tribes living in the geographical area ranging from British Columbia to southern Alaska. Those connections were cherished to the highest degree, and from time to time, a potlatch was staged to proclaim and explain them to an invited audience. Blending sacred and secular display of wealth, the potlatch was essentially a declaration of status—validated by the participation of the guests. Singing, dancing, feasting, and the distribution of goods were all part of the proceedings, and much of the celebration was festive. But other parts of the ceremony—a recapitulation of selfhood through song and dance, the wearing of crests, and the recitation of legends—were sacred. Fittingly, the very institution was rooted in the deep past.

Potlatches have changed little over the centuries although certain aspects of the ceremony have evolved to conform to the demands of modern life. These gatherings, which once could take several years to plan and prepare, now require only one year of advance work. And because most participants have full-time jobs, modern potlatches last only a day, rather than several days or a week as they did in the past. Guests today are more likely to arrive in motorized fishing boats than in cedar canoes, and may receive coffee mugs, luggage, towels, and cash in addition to the more traditional Indian-made artworks.

Above: *A Chilkat blanket, with handwoven designs, remains one of the most treasured of all Kwakiutl family heirlooms and potlatch gifts*

Left: *Lakich'inei pole in Sitka, Alaska, bearing Tlingit legends*

102

A POTLATCH CELEBRATION

*T*lingit guests in Sitka, Alaska, wear traditional dance costumes in preparation for a potlatch. These events traditionally began with several days of singing and dancing competitions between clans.

103

Northwest Coast Tsimshian dance apron displays beaver symbol

KWAKIUTL DANCERS

Wearing masks representing animal spirits, Kwakiutl dancers perform at a winter ceremony in a photograph taken by Edward Curtis in 1910. The Kwakiutl believe that spirits take over the bodies of the dancers during the rite and endow those mortals with awesome powers.

Nineteenth-century mask of a whale used in potlatch Peace Dance

LOST NINSTINTS VILLAGE
Queen Charlotte Islands

A ncient Haida totems of an abandoned Ninstints village in British Columbia, Canada.

107

Haida Thunderbird carving

THE GIFT OF DANCE

Long ago, according to a tale related by the Kiowa of the southern Plains, a warrior was returning from a raid against distant enemies when he became separated from his companions and had to find his way back home. The summer sun beat down fiercely, and the path he followed over the rolling prairie was hard and dry. Tormented by thirst, he consoled himself with thoughts of the welcome that awaited him from his friends and family members in camp, which lay far beyond the horizon.

Then, as the sun dipped toward the west, he heard a voice nearby, chanting a song as clear and as fresh as a murmuring stream. Drawn by the mysterious music, the warrior climbed to the top of a ridge and peered over the rim. There below, he saw "a beautiful red wolf at the bottom of a grassy ravine," in the words of Kiowa storyteller James Auchiah. "Red Wolf held in his right paw a gourd that he shook with a pulsating movement. His body moved rhythmically up and down in tempo with the beautiful songs pouring from his long, lean throat."

108

The warrior stood entranced on the hilltop through the night, drinking in song after song. When dawn arrived, Red Wolf spoke to his delighted listener. "I have given you a new dance with many beautiful songs," he explained. "This is a gift for you to take to your people."

Renewed by this miraculous encounter, the warrior continued his journey and reached the Kiowa encampment before the day was out. There he told his people of the gift of Red Wolf. The songs and dances he passed along to them became part of a ceremony called the Gourd Dance, performed by the tribe each summer.

In honor of the lone warrior who beheld Red Wolf, the ritual was entrusted to a society of respected hunters and soldiers. Each year, those men would begin the dance, but after a while, women would join in, for the occasion celebrated both bravery and beauty—the power and grace that came to all Kiowa who kept faith with their ancestral powers. As the drum thundered and the songs poured forth, the spirits of the dancers and of all those in attendance took flight and soared. The Kiowa never failed to honor the creature who taught them this stirring ritual of renewal. "To show their appreciation to Red Wolf," notes the storyteller, the dancers to this day end each song "with a wolf cry and a special shake of their gourds."

109

Dance plays an important role in Indian spirit seeking

THE TESTIMONY OF DANCE

Since ancient times, dance has been a way for Indians to tell of their traditions and affirm their beliefs. Sacred observances such as the Sun Dance once brought entire tribes together to testify as one in spectacular demonstrations of fervor and finery. Among the Kiowa, all those on hand "wore splendid things—beautiful buckskin and beads," related an elder called Kosahn. "The chiefs wore necklaces, and their pendants shone like the sun."

These great ceremonies declined during the reservation era, but Native Americans never stopped dancing. Tribal members continue to gather at powwows to dance and display their costumes. Roused by the beat of the drum and the spirit of the songs, the dancers leap, twist, and weave their way through intricate steps, bringing the legends of their people to life.

Above: *Eagle head dance stick*

Left: *A Stoney Indian in ceremonial dress*

112

Above: *Navajo Traditional Men's dancer at Albuquerque, New Mexico powwow* Right: *A Blood/Yakima powwow dancer*
Following pages: *A Stoney Indian performs a traditional dance at an Alberta powwow*

Above: *Traditional dance by a Crow Indian at the Standoff powwow in Alberta*

Left: *A Chippewa/Shoshone powwow dancer at Browning Indian Days in Montana* Following pages: *Otoe/Pawnee dancers perform the Shield Dance*

120

A Comanche Women's Fancy Shawl dancer at the Red Earth powwow

ALL MY RELATIONS

It is a sunny, clear day outside, almost hot, and a slight breeze comes through the room from the front door. We sit at the table and talk. As is usual in an Indian household, food preparation began as soon as we arrived and now there is the snap of potatoes frying in the black skillet, the sweet smell of white bread overwhelming even the grease, and the welcome black coffee. A ringer washer stands against the wall of the kitchen, and the counter space is taken up with dishes, pans, and boxes of food.

I am asked if I still read books and I admit that I do. Reading is not "traditional" and education has long been suspect in communities that were broken, in part, by that system, but we laugh at my confession because a television set plays in the next room.

In the living room there are two single beds. People from reservations, travelers needing help, are frequent guests here. The man who will put together the ceremony I have come to request sits on one, dozing. A girl takes him a plate of food. He eats. He is a man I have respected for many years, for his commitment to the people, for his intelligence, for his spiritual and political involvement in concerns vital to Indian people and nations. Next to him sits a girl eating potato chips, and from this room we hear the sounds of the freeway.

After eating and sitting, it is time for me to talk to him, to tell him why we have come here. I have brought him tobacco and he nods and listens as I tell him about the help we need.

I know this telling is the first part of the ceremony, my part in it. It is a story, really, that finds its way into language, and story is at the very crux of healing, at the heart of every ceremony and ritual in the older America.

The ceremony itself includes not just our own prayers and stories of what brought us to it, but includes the unspoken records of history, the mythic past, and all the other lives connected to ours, our family, nations, and all other creatures.

I am sent home to prepare. I tie fifty tobacco ties, green. This I do with Bull Durham tobacco, squares of cotton which are tied with twine and left strung together. These are called prayer ties. I spend the time preparing in silence and alone. Each tie has a prayer in it. I will also need wood for the fire, meat, and bread for food.

On the day of the ceremony, we meet in the next town and leave my car in public parking. My daughters and I climb into the back seat. The man who will help us is drumming and singing in front of us. His wife drives and chants. He doesn't speak. He is moving between the worlds, beginning already to step over the boundaries of what we think, in daily and ordinary terms, is real and present. He is already feeling, hearing, knowing what else is there, that which is around us daily but too often unacknowledged, a larger life than our own small ones. We pass billboards and little towns and gas stations. An eagle flies overhead. It is "a good sign," we all agree. We stop to watch it.

We stop again, later, at a convenience store to fill the gas tank and to buy soda. The leader still drums and is silent. He is going into the drum, going into the center, even here as we drive west on the highway, even with our conversations about other people, family.

It is a hot balmy day, and by the time we reach the site where the ceremony is to take place, we are slow and sleepy with the brightness and warmth of the sun. In some tribes, men and women participate in separate sweat lodge ceremonies, but here, men, women, and children all come together to sweat. The children are cooling off in the creek. A woman stirs the fire that lives inside a circle of black rocks, pots beside her, a jar of oil, a kettle, a can of coffee. The leaves of the trees are thick and green.

In the background, the sweat lodge structure stands. Birds are on it. It is still skeletal. A woman and man are beginning to place old rugs and blankets over the bent cottonwood frame. A great fire is already burning, and the lava stones that will be the source of heat for the sweat are being fired in it.

A few people sit outside on lawn chairs and cast-off couches that have the stuffing coming out. We sip coffee and talk about the food, about recent events. A man tells us that a friend gave him money for a new car. The creek sounds restful. Another man falls asleep. My young daughter splashes in the water. Heat waves rise up behind us from the fire that is preparing the stones. My tobacco ties are placed inside, on the framework of the lodge.

By late afternoon we are ready, one at a time, to enter the enclosure. The hot lava stones are placed inside. They remind us of earth's red and fiery core, and of the spark inside all life. After the flap, which serves as a door, is closed, water is poured over the stones and the hot steam rises around us. In a sweat lodge ceremony,

122

the entire world is brought inside the enclosure. The soft odor of smoking cedar accompanies this arrival of every-

thing. It is all called in. The animals come from the warm and sunny distances. Water from dark lakes is there.

Wind. Young, lithe willow branches bent overhead remember their lives rooted in ground, the sun their leaves

took in. They remember that minerals and water rose up their trunks, and birds nested in their leaves, and that

planets turned above their brief, slender lives. The thunder clouds travel in from far regions of earth. Wind arrives

from the four directions. It has moved through caves and breathed through our bodies. It is the same air elk have

inhaled, air that passed through the lungs of a grizzly bear. The sky is there, with all the stars whose lights we

see long after the stars themselves have gone back to nothing. It is a place grown intense and holy. It is a place

of immense community and of humbled solitude; we sit together in our aloneness and speak, one at a time, our

deepest language of need, hope, loss, and survival. We remember that all things are connected.

Remembering this is the purpose of the ceremony. It is part of a healing and restoration. It is the mend-

ing of a broken connection between us and the rest. The participants in a ceremony say the words, "All my rela-

tions," before and after we pray; those words create a relationship with other people, with animals, with the land.

To have health it is necessary to keep all these relations in mind.

The intention of a ceremony is to put a person back together by restructuring the human mind. This reor-

ganization is accomplished by a kind of inner map, a geography of the human spirit and the rest of the world. We

make whole our broken-off pieces of self and world. Within ourselves, we bring together the fragments of our lives

123

Dakota Sioux sweat lodge

in a sacred act of renewal, and we reestablish our connections with others. The ceremony is a point of return. It takes us toward the place of balance, our place in the community of all things. It is an event that sets us back upright. But it is not a finished thing. The real ceremony begins where the formal one ends, when we take up a new way, our minds and hearts filled with the vision of earth that holds us within it, in compassionate relationship to and with our world.

We speak. We sing. We swallow water and breathe smoke. By the end of the ceremony, it is as if skin contains land and birds. The places within us have become filled. As inside the enclosure of the lodge, the animals and ancestors move into the human body, into skin and blood. The land merges with us. The stones come to dwell inside the person. Gold rolling hills take up residence, their tall grasses blowing. The red light of canyons is there. The black skies of night that wheel above our heads come to live inside the skull. We who easily grow apart from the world are returned to the great store of life all around us and there is the deepest sense of being at home here in this intimate kinship. There is no real aloneness. There is solitude and the nurturing silence that is relationship with ourselves, but even then we are part of something larger.

After a sweat lodge ceremony, the enclosure is abandoned. Quieter now, we prepare to drive home. We pack up the kettles, the coffee pot. The prayer ties are placed in nearby trees. Some of the other people prepare to go to work, go home, or cook a dinner. We drive home. Everything returns to ordinary use. A spider weaves a web from one of the cottonwood poles to another. Crows sit inside the framework. It's evening. The crickets are singing. All my relations.

LINDA HOGAN, CHICKASAW

124

THE HEALING WAYS OF THE NAVAJO

The essence of Navajo culture is the maintenance of *hózhó*, a term that corresponds roughly to the English word *harmony*. Wrong behavior of any kind can upset the delicate balance between the good and evil powers in the Navajo universe and bring sickness and misfortune to the transgressor. To restore the disrupted order and treat the disease, the Navajo possess myriad ancient healing ceremonies, called Chant Ways. Each Way is so complex that a practitioner, or singer, rarely masters more than two of them in a lifetime. A single Way can last up to nine days or longer and involves many prayers, medicines, and offerings, as well as hundreds of songs that recount Navajo history. The ceremony may also involve the creation of several sand paintings, selected from the dozen used in the Chant Ways.

These paintings are made primarily of colored sandstone ground into a fine powder. The singer and his assistants trickle the pigment onto a bed of fresh sand on the floor of the patient's dwelling. The patient, bearing a gift of cornmeal, sits on the painting, facing east, the direction from which all Navajo blessings come. Attracted by the ceremony, the relevant supernatural powers enter the painting and make it their home. If the powers are pleased, the patient is cured. Afterward, the singer's assistants ceremonially dispose of the sand, which has absorbed the evil that caused the disharmony. Sand paintings actually used in the healing rituals are considered too sacred to be photographed.

126

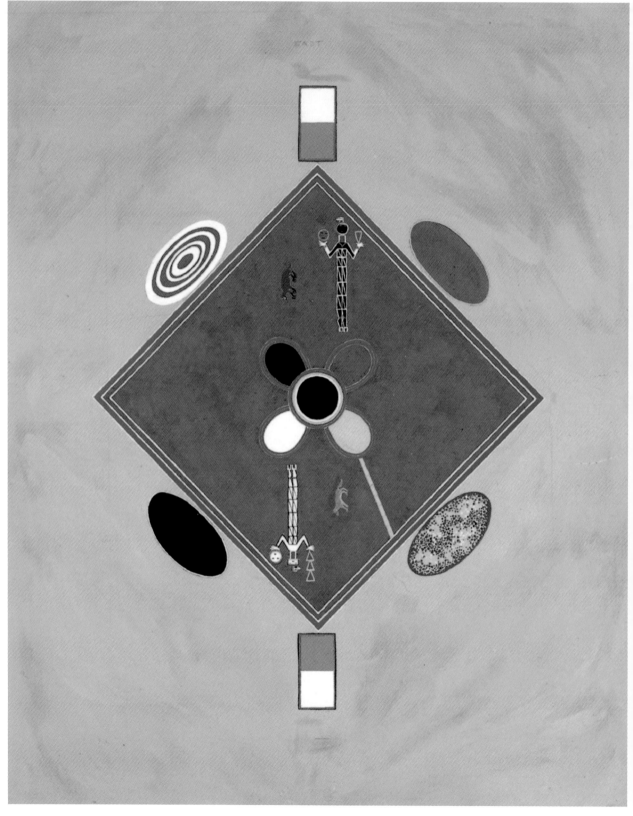

Blessingway

Earthway

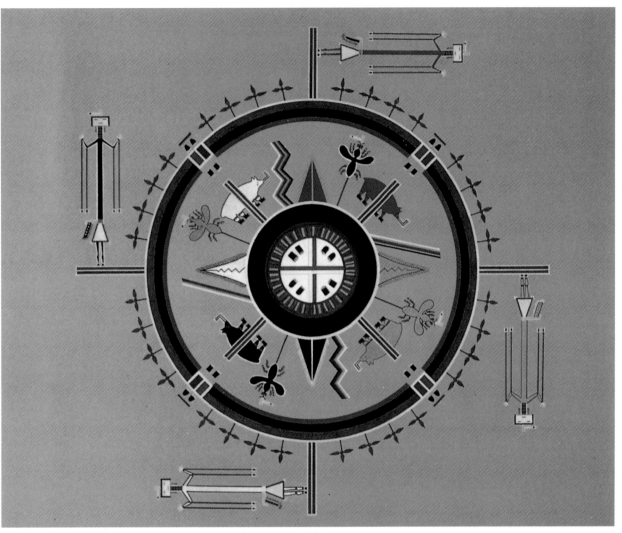

BLESSINGWAY AND EARTHWAY

Bears, thought by the Navajo to possess healing powers, appear in each of the quadrants of the Earthway sand painting (above), part of a ritual intended to restore a woman to harmony with the world. The sand painting of the Blessingway (left), the most important Navajo ceremony, shows their homeland as a square flanked by ovals representing the four sacred mountains. Inside the square are Changing Woman, who represents nature and the mystery of reproduction, and her sister, White Shell Woman, who represents water.

Shootingway

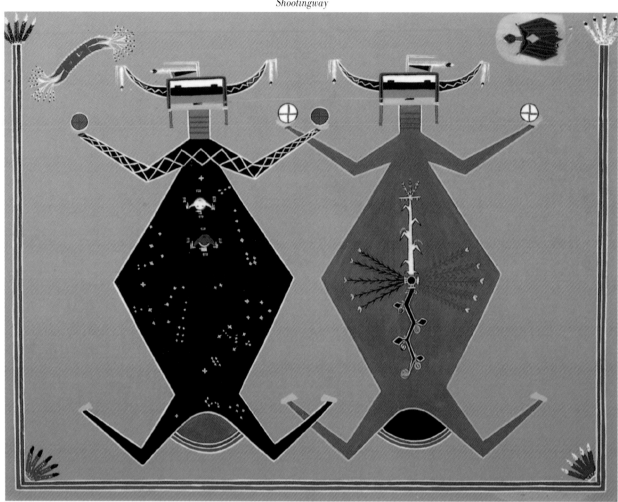

128

SHOOTINGWAY AND WATERWAY

T he Waterway
(right), *Emergence Lake—the route through
which the Navajo ascended to this world—
occupies the center of the sand painting. In
this depiction of the Waterway Ceremony,
stalks from the four sacred plants—corn,
squash, beans, and tobacco—radiate from its
sides. The elongated figures are Rain People,
carrying clouds. In Shootingway (above),
Father Sky and Mother Earth, two of the most
powerful Navajo deities, dominate in a design
made on the fourth day of a healing ceremony
that addressed respiratory and gastrointestinal
ailments.*

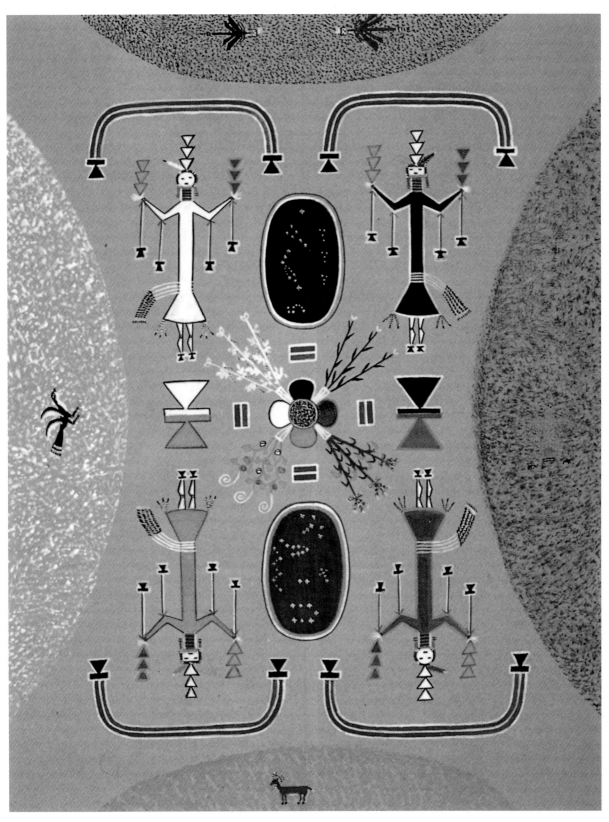

Waterway

WHITE BUFFALO WOMAN

One summer so long ago that nobody knows how long, the Oceti-Sakowin, the seven sacred council fires of the Lakota Oyate, the nation, came together and camped. The sun shone all the time, but there was no game and the people were starving. Every day they sent scouts to look for game, but the scouts found nothing.

Among the bands assembled were the Itazipcho, the Without-Bows, who had their own camp circle under their chief, Standing Hollow Horn. Early one morning the chief sent two of his young men to hunt for game. They searched everywhere but could find nothing. Seeing a high hill, they decided to climb it in order to look over the whole country. Halfway up, they saw something coming toward them from far off, but the figure was floating instead of walking. From this they knew that the person was *wakan*, holy.

At first they could make out only a small moving speck and had to squint to see that it was a human form. But as it came nearer, they realized that it was a beautiful young woman, with two round, red dots of face paint on her cheeks. She wore a wonderful white buckskin outfit, tanned until it shone a long way in the sun. It was embroidered with sacred and marvelous designs of porcupine quill, in radiant colors no ordinary woman could have made. This wakan stranger was Ptesan-Wi, White Buffalo Woman. In her hands she carried a large bundle and a fan of sage leaves. She wore her blueblack hair loose except for a strand at the left side, which was tied up with buffalo fur. Her eyes shone dark and sparkling, with great power in them.

Painted buffalo skull

The two young men looked at her open-mouthed. One was awestruck, but the other desired her body and stretched his hand out to touch her. This woman was *lila wakan*, very sacred, and could not be treated with disrespect. Lightning instantly struck the brash young man and burned him up, so that only a small heap of blackened bones was left.

To the other scout who had behaved rightly, the White Buffalo Woman said: "Good things I am bringing, something holy to your nation. A message I carry for your people from the buffalo nation. Go back to the camp and tell the people to prepare for my arrival. Tell your chief to put up a medicine lodge with twenty-four poles. Let it be made holy for my coming."

This young hunter returned to the camp. He told the chief, he told the people, what the sacred woman had commanded. The chief told the *eyapaha*, the crier, and the crier went through the camp circle calling: "Someone sacred is coming. A holy woman approaches. Make all things ready for her." So the people put up the big medicine tipi and waited. After four days they saw the White Buffalo Woman approaching, carrying her bundle before her. The chief, Standing Hollow Horn, invited her to enter the medicine lodge. She went in and circled the interior sun-wise, or clockwise. The chief addressed her respectfully, saying: "Sister, we are glad you have come to instruct us."

She told him what she wanted done. In the center of the tipi they were to put up a *wanka wakan*, a sacred altar, made of red earth, with a buffalo skull and a three-stick rack for a holy thing she was bringing. They did what she directed, and she traced a design with her finger on the smoothed earth of the altar. She showed them how to do all this, then circled the lodge again sunwise. Halting before the chief, she now opened the bundle. The holy thing it contained was the *chanunpa*, the sacred pipe. She held it out to the people and let them look at it. She was grasp-

131

ing the stem with her right hand and the bowl with her left, and thus the pipe has been held ever since.

Again the chief spoke, saying: "Sister, we are glad. We have had no meat for some time. All we can give you is water." They dipped some *wacanga*, sweet grass, into a skin bag of water and gave it to her, and to this day the people dip sweet grass or an eagle wing in water and sprinkle it on a person to be purified.

The White Buffalo Woman showed the people how to use the pipe. She filled it with *chan-shasha*, red willow-bark tobacco. She walked around the lodge four times after the manner of Anpetu-Wi, the great sun. This represented the circle without end, the sacred hoop, the road of life. The woman placed a dry buffalo chip on the fire and lit the pipe with it. This was *peta-owihankeshni*, the fire without end, the flame to be passed on from generation to generation. She told them that the smoke rising from the bowl was Tunkashila's breath, the breath of the great Grandfather Mystery.

The White Buffalo Woman showed the people the right way to pray, the right words and the right gestures. She taught them how to sing the pipe-filling song and how to lift the pipe up to the sky, toward Grandfather, and down toward Grandmother Earth, to Unci, and then to the four directions of the universe.

"With this holy pipe," she said, "you will walk like a living prayer. With your feet resting upon the earth and the pipestem reaching into the sky, your body forms a living bridge between the Sacred Beneath and the Sacred Above. Wakan Tanka smiles upon us, because now

Mandan communal pipe collected by Lewis and Clark, 1804-1806

we are as one: earth, sky, all living things, the two-legged, the four-legged, the winged ones, the trees, the grasses. The pipe holds them all together.

132

"Look at this bowl," said the White Buffalo Woman. "Its stone represents the buffalo, but also the flesh and blood of the red man. The buffalo represents the universe and the four directions, because he stands on four legs, for the four ages of creation. The buffalo was put in the West by Wakan Tanka at the making of the world, to hold back the waters. Every year he loses one hair, and in every one of the four ages he loses a leg. The sacred hoop will end when all the hair and legs of the great buffalo are gone, and the water comes back to cover the earth.

The wooden stem of this *chanunpa* stands for all that grows on the earth. Twelve feathers hanging from where the stem (the backbone) joins the bowl (the skull) are from Wanblee Galeshka, the spotted eagle, the very sacred bird who is the Great Spirit's messenger and the wisest of all flying ones. You are joined to all things of the universe, for they all cry out to Tunkashila. Look at the bowl: engraved in it are seven circles of various sizes. They stand for the seven sacred ceremonies you will practice with this pipe, and for the Oceti-Sakowin, the seven sacred campfires of our Lakota nation."

The White Buffalo Woman then spoke to the women, telling them that it was the work of their hands and the fruit of their bodies which kept the people alive. "You are from the mother earth," she told them. "What you are doing is as great as what the warriors do."

And therefore the sacred pipe binds men and women together in a circle of love. It is the one holy object in the making of which both men and women have a hand. The men carve the bowl and make the stem; the women decorate it with bands of colored porcupine quills. When a man takes a wife, they both hold the pipe at the same time and red trade cloth is wound around their hands, thus tying them together for life.

The White Buffalo Woman had many things for her Lakota sisters in her sacred womb bag—corn, *wasna* (pemmican), wild turnip. She taught them how to make the hearth fire. She filled a buffalo paunch with cold water and dropped a red-hot stone into it. "This way you shall cook the corn and the meat," she told them.

The White Buffalo Woman also talked to the children, because they have an understanding beyond their years. She told them that what their fathers and mothers did was for them, that their parents could remember being little once, and that they, the children, would grow up to have little ones of their own. She told them: "You are the coming generation, that's why you are the most important and precious ones. Some day you will hold this pipe and smoke it. Some day you will pray with it."

She spoke once more to all the people: "The pipe is alive; it is a red being showing you a red life and a red road. And this is the first ceremony for which you will use the pipe. You will use it to keep the soul of a dead person, because through it you can talk to Wakan Tanka, the Great Mystery Spirit. The day a human dies is always a sacred day. The day when the soul is released to the Great Spirit is another. Four women will become sacred on such a day. They will be the ones to cut the sacred tree—the *can-wakan*—for the Sun Dance."

She spoke one last time to Standing Hollow Horn, the chief, saying, "Remember: this pipe is very sacred. Respect it and it will take you to the end of the road. The four ages of creation are in me; I am the four ages. I will come to see you in every generation cycle. I shall come back to you."

The sacred woman took leave of the people, saying: "*Toksha ake wacinyanktin ktelo*—I shall see you again."

The people saw her walking off in the same direction from which she had come, outlined against the red ball of the setting sun. As she went, she stopped and rolled over four times. The first time, she turned into a black buffalo; the second into a brown one; the third into a red one; and finally, the fourth time she rolled over, she turned into a white female buffalo calf. A white buffalo is the most sacred thing you could ever encounter. The White Buffalo Woman disappeared over the horizon. Sometime she might come back. As soon as she had vanished, buffalo in great herds appeared, allowing themselves to be killed so that the people might survive.

133

LEGEND OF THE PIPE—AS TOLD BY LAME DEER, 1967

SACRED SMOKE RISING

For the eastern Algonquian, as for most Native Americans, tobacco is a sacred substance that some believe originated from the bones of a mythical first mother. Down through the years, the plant has played an important role in Indian ritual. Before embarking on any venture, Algonquian traditionally made an offering of tobacco, sometimes as the crumbled leaf but most often smoked. The rising smoke is visible evidence of human desire for contact with the spirit powers above and within the natural world. The gesture signifies commitment and makes a request for support. In relationships with fellow humans, the sharing of a pipe suggests the trust and intimacy of a common purpose.

Tobacco was so central to life that a man always carried a pipe and pouch with him. The oldest pipes were made of clay or soapstone and sometimes had animal or spirit effigies carved on the bowls. Others had reed stems up to six feet long. The men cultivated the tobacco plants in special gardens set apart from the food crops tended by the women. For a milder smoke, they mixed the crushed tobacco leaves with the leaves of other plants, such as sumac, and the inner bark of dogwood and cedar trees. Each tribe had its own formula. The Algonquian called such a blend *kinnikinnick*, a word meaning "that which is mixed."

135

Above: *A Sioux burns sweet grass before embarking on a vision quest*
Left: *Crow Indians smoke long ceremonial pipes to communicate with the spirit world*

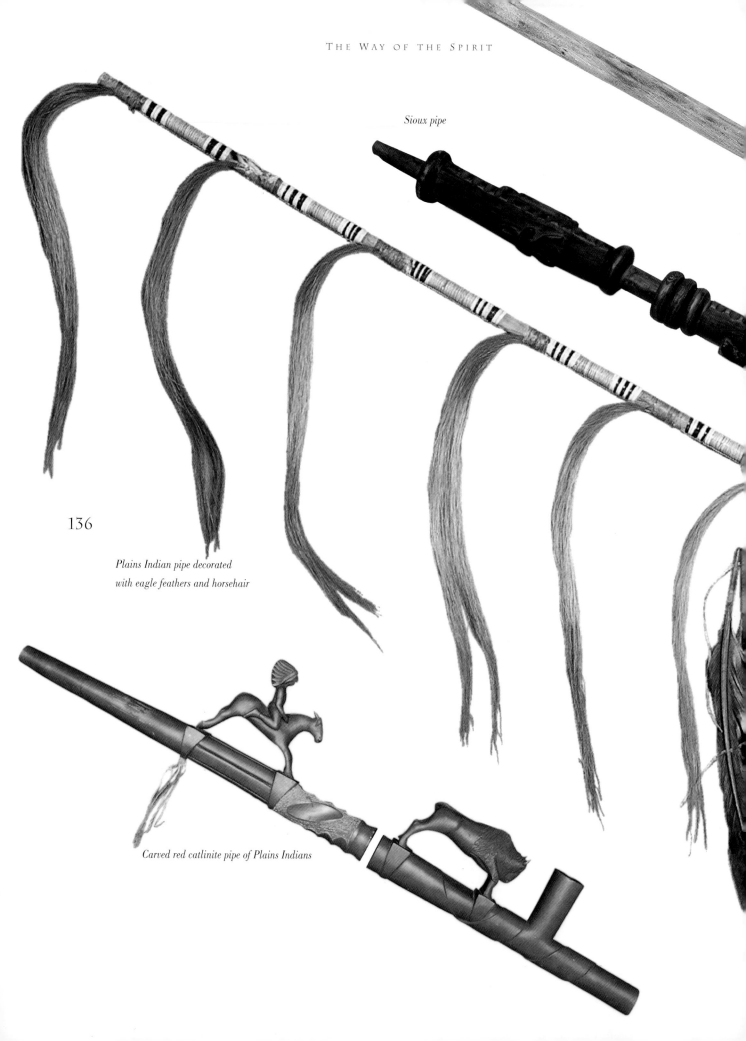

Sioux pipe

136

*Plains Indian pipe decorated
with eagle feathers and horsehair*

Carved red catlinite pipe of Plains Indians

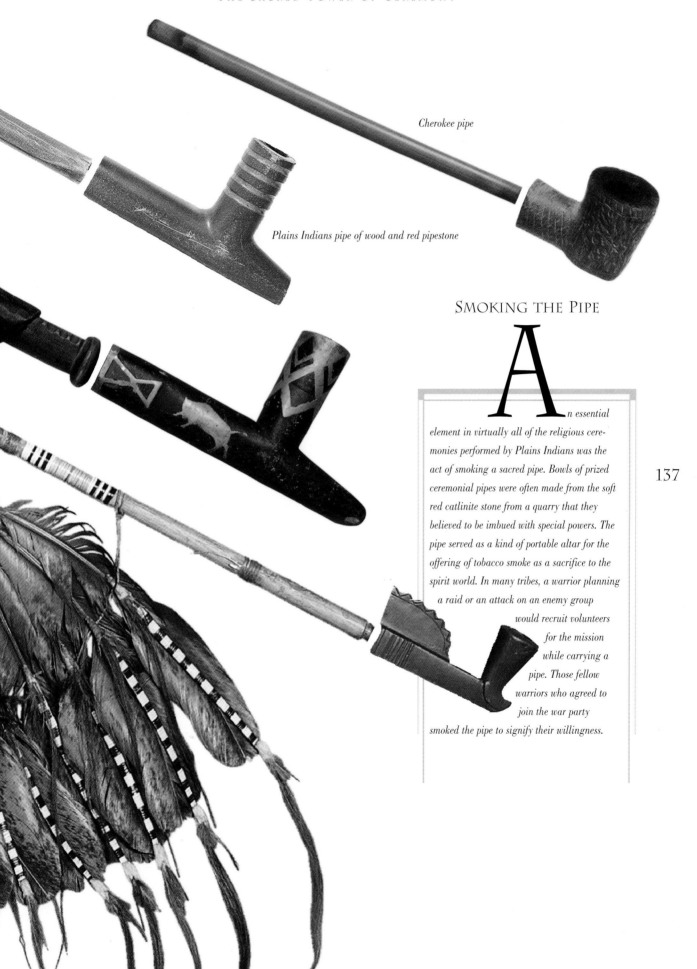

Cherokee pipe

Plains Indians pipe of wood and red pipestone

SMOKING THE PIPE

An essential element in virtually all of the religious ceremonies performed by Plains Indians was the act of smoking a sacred pipe. Bowls of prized ceremonial pipes were often made from the soft red catlinite stone from a quarry that they believed to be imbued with special powers. The pipe served as a kind of portable altar for the offering of tobacco smoke as a sacrifice to the spirit world. In many tribes, a warrior planning a raid or an attack on an enemy group would recruit volunteers for the mission while carrying a pipe. Those fellow warriors who agreed to join the war party smoked the pipe to signify their willingness.

137

SMOKE CEREMONY

Blackfeet Indians burn foot-long braids of sweet grass (Anthoxanthum odoratum) *to create a sacred, purifying incense for daily prayers and special ceremonies. The smoking bag (right) has three pockets to hold a pipe, tobacco, and fire-starting materials. The stone pipe bowl (below) has an opening for the wooden stem through the bear's back and hind legs.*

Stone pipe bowl

138

Micmac smoking bag

Blackfeet sweet grass braid for burning

PRAYER TO THE GHOST

Here it is, the tobacco.

I am certain that you, O ghost, are not very far away, that in fact you are standing

right in back of me, waiting for me to reach you the pipe and tobacco, that you

might take it along with you, that likewise you are waiting for your food to take on your journey.

However, four nights you will have to remain here.

Now here are those things, and in return we ask you to act as

mediator [between the spirits and us]. You have made us long for you, and therefore

see to it that all those things that belonged to you and that you would have enjoyed had

you lived longer—victories on the warpath, earthly possessions, and life—that all

these things you leave behind for us to enjoy. This you must ask for us as you travel along.

This also I ask of you: do not cause us to follow you soon;

do not cause your brothers any fear.

I have now lit the pipe for you.

WINNEBAGO

139

WHERE SPIRITS
DWELL

Long ago, according to the Nootka of Vancouver Island, a chief visited his salmon trap day after day and was dismayed to find it always empty. Realizing that someone was stealing his fish, he hid in the bushes and kept watch. At length, a *winatshisht,* or "supernatural canoe," approached with a crew of ten *ya'ai,* manlike spirits with hairy bodies and feathered ears. The chief fainted from fright and did not regain consciousness until after the spirits had paddled off downstream. Summoning his courage, he resumed his vigil. The ya'ai eventually reappeared, towing a whale behind their canoe. When the spirits stopped to make camp on the far side of the river, the chief let out a ritual scream that transformed them and the whale into foam. He carefully scooped up the frothy bubbles, knowing they contained the spiritual

Above: *Salmon rattle used by Tlingit Indians to honor the salmon in rituals celebrating the annual salmon harvest*

Left: *A Pacific Northwest old growth forest*

essence of the ya'ai and the whale. With this potent substance in his possession, he confidently moved his people down to the seashore and introduced them to a new way of life—whale hunting. The Nootka thrived at their new pursuit, and none more so than the chief, who killed one or two whales every time he ventured out to sea.

The story of that ancestral encounter is but one of countless legends linking the Indians of the Pacific Northwest to the supernatural. Like Native Americans of other areas, these coastal people have traditionally perceived the world as populated with a host of mysterious powers that dwell amid the region's thick forests and rugged mountains, its many rivers and streams, and in the skies and ocean depths. Indeed, a sense of the sacred permeated all aspects of their lives. Long ago, the paths of spirits and humans often intersected, allowing the Indians to acquire special skills, such as the Nootka's ability to hunt whales. Some of those skills have been passed on to later generations, and new skills have been gained, since the potency of the spirits remains undiminished, even if encounters with them are less frequent today.

According to ancient belief, the spirits were also responsible for many natural phenomena—the changing of the seasons, the movement of the sun across the sky, the maintaining of the earth in a state of balance. Most of these beings were said to be human in essence, if they were visualized at all. Many took on the guise of animals, birds, or fish, although they reverted to human shape when they returned to their own lands.

The ranks of the spirits included a number of nightmarish beings that preyed on humans—mountain lions, for example, that walked backward and killed with a flick of their lancelike tails, and shadowy trees that claimed the life of anyone who dared look at them. Nootka tradition relates the story of one

Woodpecker dance baton

142

spirit that changed into ten different kinds of birds; humans encountering this creature died if they failed to watch the full succession of metamorphoses.

Although spirits inhabited specific sites, such as a lake, a mountain, or a place where violent ocean currents swirled, the geography of the supernatural realm was generally ill-defined, and the boundaries between the natural and spirit world were often uncertain.

Haida Thunderbird image

143

Maidu headdress plume

SPIRITS OF THE NORTH

The fabulous mythological creatures that shamans encountered in dreams or in the course of their flights to the spirit world were rendered tangible to their communities through the use of the masks that were used in ceremonial dances. Created either by the shaman himself, or by a skilled craftsman in accordance with the shaman's instructions, these colorful and imaginative masks represent the powerful deities believed to control natural phenomena or the spirits, or *inuas*, of game animals and other creatures.

Masks generally were carved from wood and ranged in size from lightweight face coverings to massive constructions as tall as a person. The latter, too heavy to be worn, were suspended from the ceilings of ceremonial houses. Masks were designed according to individual impulse and inspiration, and no two were exactly alike. Many of them, however, incorporated artistic conventions that identified them as specific beings, such as *tungat* (plural of *tungak*), the spirits who controlled the supply of game animals. Tungat were frequently depicted with motifs suggesting the moon, where they were said to reside. When a shaman wore a mask, its spirit was thought to dwell within him, conferring its special powers. Most masks were used for only a single performance or celebration. Then, their powers having been exhausted, they were burned, buried, or sometimes sold.

145

Above: *Inuit Worm-man mask*

Left: *The human face of a seabird's inua peers from the creature's open beak*

Tomalik, the wind maker spirit

DEITIES OF WIND AND WATER

The winter and summer winds are said to blow through the hollow tubes fitted through the mouth and forehead of Tomalik, the wind maker spirit. White feathers evoke scudding clouds and soaring seabirds. The water deity Walaunuk wears a curved tube with wooden disks that represent air bubbles. The Inuit observed the air bubbles that rose to the surface from seal bladders ceremonially submerged; they foretold success or failure in hunting and fishing.

146

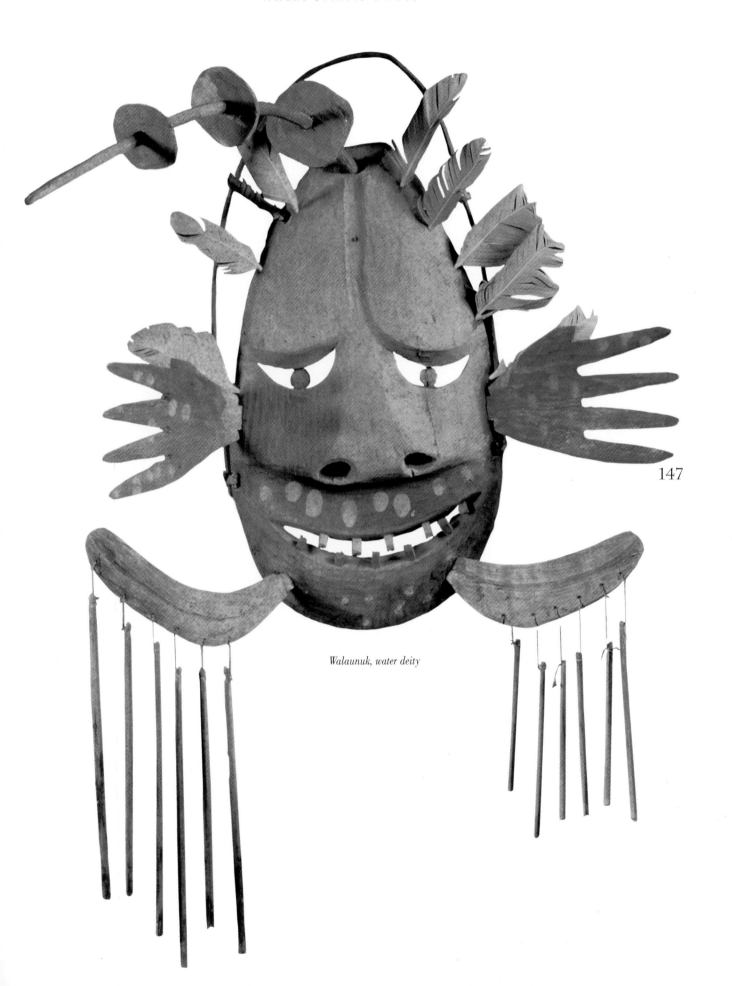

147

Walaunuk, water deity

SHAPES OF SPIRIT CREATURES

148

The hinged door on this otter spirit mask opens to reveal the spirit's human face, something all inuas possessed. The two bentwood hoops symbolize the otter's universe. The spirit mask of a shaman (far right), *from Alaska's lower Kuskokwim River region, depicts his torso split open to reveal his internal organs as he sits astride a beaver spirit.*

Otter spirit mask

Shaman spirit mask

SPIRITS OF THE PACIFIC COAST

For Pacific Northwest tribes, the world teems with spirits that dwell within every facet of nature: great whales, spawning fish, and the chill waters that carry them; raven, wind, sun, and all the powers and residents of the sky; the mist-shrouded forests, and the sundry creatures that stalk their quarry or seek shelter from pursuit in the deep shadows.

A vital force pervades every fiber of existence, from stones that can only tumble down the flanks of mountains to the echoes that fill the valleys when they fall. And for benevolent spirits, there are corresponding faces reflecting the interwoven genealogies of man, animal, earth, and their supernatural forebears. The world of these tribes abounds in faces, whether worked into household articles or gazing out from towering poles, in amulets, or crafted artifacts, but none of these stylized visages hold the power that resides in masks.

Masterpieces of the carver's skill and inspiration, masks enable dancers and shamans to personify the deities, creatures, and forces evoked during the sacred ceremonies and healing rituals. No two masks are the same, yet each bears features that for generations have faithfully invoked the presence of a spiritual guest.

151

Above: *Ceremonial mask of a killer whale sometimes worn in a mourning ritual that precedes winter ceremonies*
Left: *The Tsimshian lunar mask opens a portal to the invisible world, where fabulous beings play out immortal dramas*

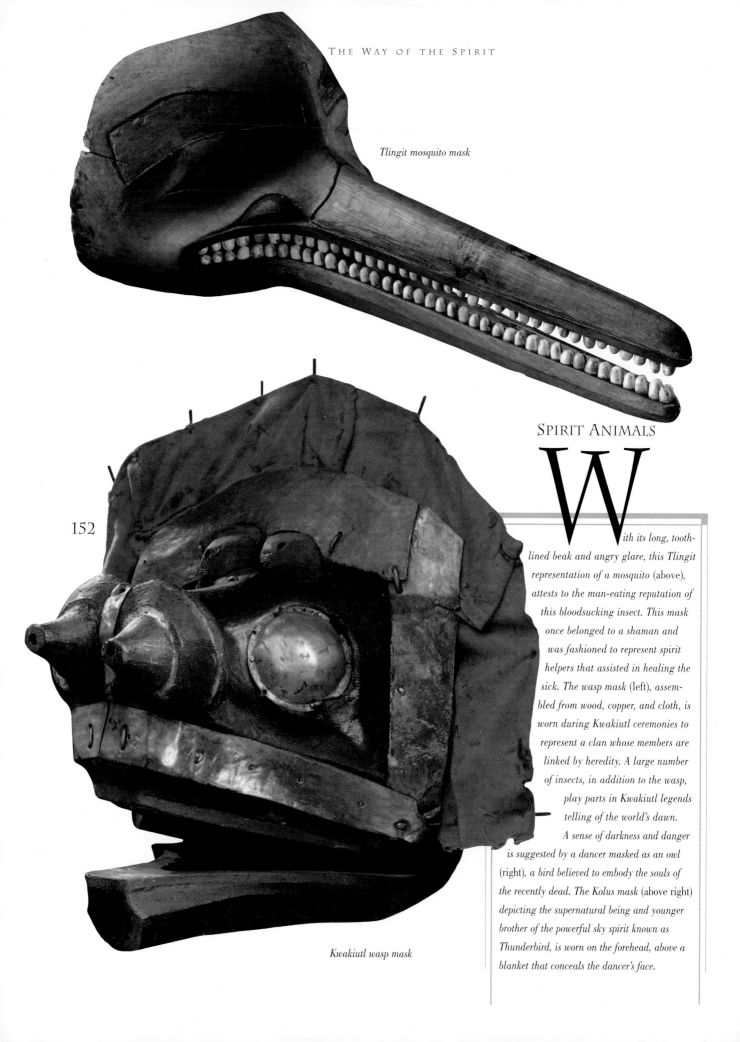

Tlingit mosquito mask

SPIRIT ANIMALS

With its long, tooth-lined beak and angry glare, this Tlingit representation of a mosquito (above), attests to the man-eating reputation of this bloodsucking insect. This mask once belonged to a shaman and was fashioned to represent spirit helpers that assisted in healing the sick. The wasp mask (left), assembled from wood, copper, and cloth, is worn during Kwakiutl ceremonies to represent a clan whose members are linked by heredity. A large number of insects, in addition to the wasp, play parts in Kwakiutl legends telling of the world's dawn.

A sense of darkness and danger is suggested by a dancer masked as an owl (right), a bird believed to embody the souls of the recently dead. The Kolus mask (above right) depicting the supernatural being and younger brother of the powerful sky spirit known as Thunderbird, is worn on the forehead, above a blanket that conceals the dancer's face.

152

Kwakiutl wasp mask

Kolus, younger brother of Thunderbird

Owl mask

153

154

THE LIFE-GIVING SUN

The Bella Coola mask shown here portrays at its center the life-giving sun. According to a legend handed down by the Bella Coola, the sun serves as a canoe for the supreme being, Althguntam, who journeys across the heavens while wearing a cloak lined with silvery salmon. The faces on the rim of the mask depict the Four Carpenters who constructed the world of the Bella Coola.

155

TALISMANS:
POTENT WITH POWER

Many Indian warriors entered into battle taking along their personal talismans. These tokens, frequently shaped like shields, assured the wearers that their guardian spirits were present, bringing with them the supernatural power needed for victory.

The talismans not only bolstered the warriors' courage, they were also believed to give a fighter's arm added strength to deflect enemy arrows. In addition, amulets that were worn prominently in the hair or around the neck served as a warning to foes that they faced not just human opponents but also the omnipotent spirits.

Badger—guardian of the south

156

Of the pueblo-dwelling Native Americans, the Zuni are particularly recognized for their faith in the power of animal fetishes to assist them in their lives. Contrary to non-Indian conceptions that human beings are superior to other living creatures, the Zuni believe that animals—with their keen senses, sharp teeth, claws, talons, stealth, and quickness—are closer to the gods than are people.

A great deal of the meaning behind the animal talismans is known only by members of the secret Zuni medicine societies. According to tribal legend, as the Zuni ancestors emerged from the underworld, the two children of the Zuni supreme being turned many of

Mole—guardian of the underworld   the most dangerous predators into stone in order to save the people from being devoured. The children allowed the hearts of the animals to continue to live inside the stone, however. It is to the spirits of these predators, captured within the tiny, palm-sized fetishes, that the Zuni

Bear—for promoting healing

Banded coyote—for harmony between a man and a woman

turn for assistance. A variety of animal fetishes are available to promote success in diverse personal and communal endeavors, including farming, marital relations, healing the sick, and, especially, the hunting of wild animals.

In keeping with tradition, fetishes are stored inside special earthenware jars where they are fed ceremonial food and water. Some even have offerings of beads or arrowheads tied to them with twine. Inside the jar, each fetish rests on a bed of soft down, its head facing the hole located at the bottom. The hole allows the fetishes to ceremonially breathe and to partake of the sacred cornmeal and water that their owner offers them as nourishment. To keep out dust, the top of the jar is usually covered with deerskin. A flat rock is then placed on top of the skin. Should the fetish fail to produce the desired results, it is considered the fault of the owner for not tending it properly.

Frog—for bringing rain

157

Zuni men carried carved fetishes, representing Zuni hunter gods who ruled the game animals, in order to ensure a successful hunt. Their choice of a talisman depended upon their intended quarry. A mountain lion fetish was preferred for hunting buffalo, elk, and deer; a coyote for mountain sheep; a wildcat or wolf for antelope; and an eagle for rabbit. The mole fetish was used to hunt small burrowing animals. By placing the mouth of the talis-

Mountain lion with arrowhead—for protection from surprise attack

man next to his own, the hunter obtained the magical breath of the hunter god, allowing him to charm his prey. At the kill, he cut open the heart of the dead animal and bathed the fetish in the warm blood to further strengthen its power.

Snake—for hunting dangerous animals

FACES OF THE DEMONS

Grotesquely tufted with hair, ghost masks figure in a most important winter ceremony, the Hamatsa Dance, performed by a society whose members claim power from a dire spirit known as Cannibal at the North End of the World. During the rites, a person being initiated into the society visits the underworld in the company of ghosts, an episode often heightened by magical effects. Sometimes the initiate will journey to the underworld by falling into a hole prepared in the floor of the ceremonial house, while other times, ghostly voices call from below via a hollow tube of kelp.

Many spirits were hostile to humans. Wild Woman of the Woods is a sleepy-eyed giantess represented with lips pursed to utter the chilling cry "Hu! Hu!" She savors tender human flesh and carries a basket used to collect small children in the course of her wanderings in the forest.

Above: *Kwakiutl Wild Woman of the Woods spirit mask*

Left: *Hamatsa Dance ghost masks*

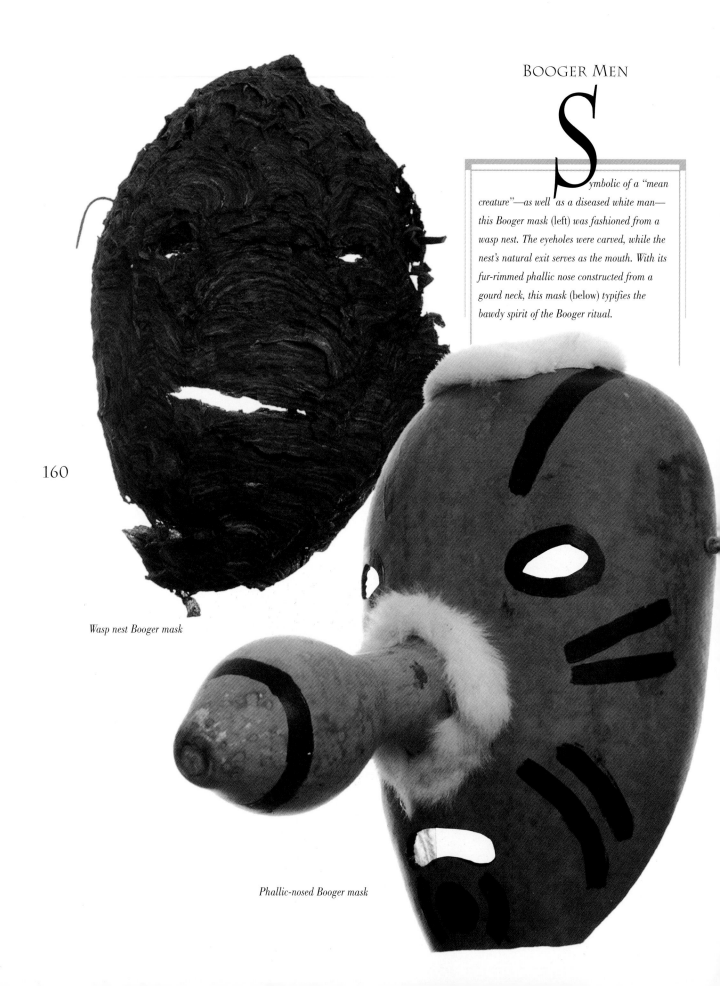

BOOGER MEN

Symbolic of a "mean creature"—as well as a diseased white man—this Booger mask (left) was fashioned from a wasp nest. The eyeholes were carved, while the nest's natural exit serves as the mouth. With its fur-rimmed phallic nose constructed from a gourd neck, this mask (below) typifies the bawdy spirit of the Booger ritual.

160

Wasp nest Booger mask

Phallic-nosed Booger mask

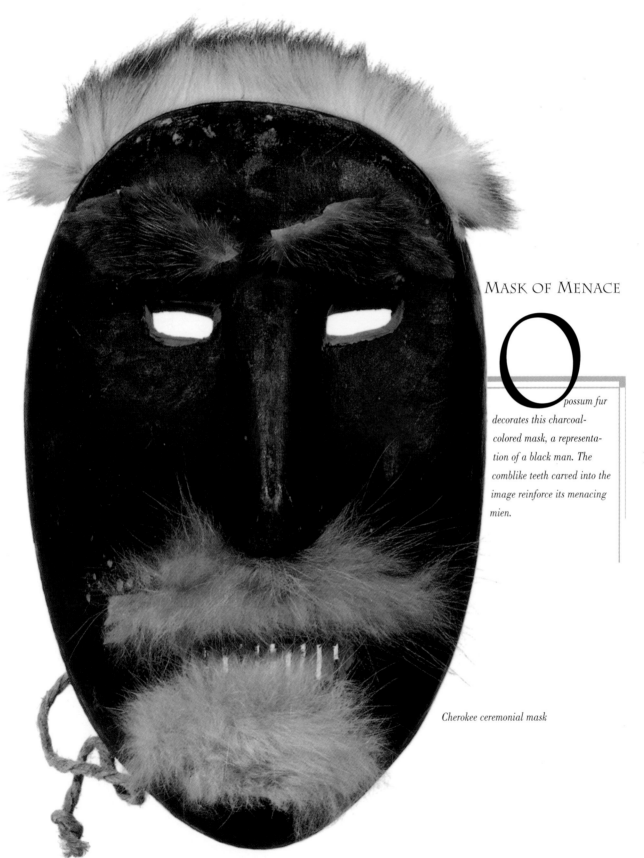

MASK OF MENACE

Opossum fur decorates this charcoal-colored mask, a representation of a black man. The comblike teeth carved into the image reinforce its menacing mien.

161

Cherokee ceremonial mask

WATER SPIRITS

*D*epicting a lake-dwelling protector spirit of the Coast Salish, this birdlike mask with protruding ears (right) is crowned by animal heads and a stand of feathers. Ownership of such masks has been restricted to select families who bring them out to sanctify important social events. The family-crest mask (far right), with its cedar bark beard, commemorates a sea monster known as Yagim, who wielded great power in the realm that supplied much of the Kwakiutl's livelihood. Legends describe Yagim as a sharklike spirit that trails behind canoes, sometimes capsizing them and devouring the humans as they flail in the waves. In a baleful mood, the monster can whip up raging storms, cause the sea to boil, and destroy whole tribes.

162

Coast Salish protector mask

163

Yagim, Kwakiutl sea monster

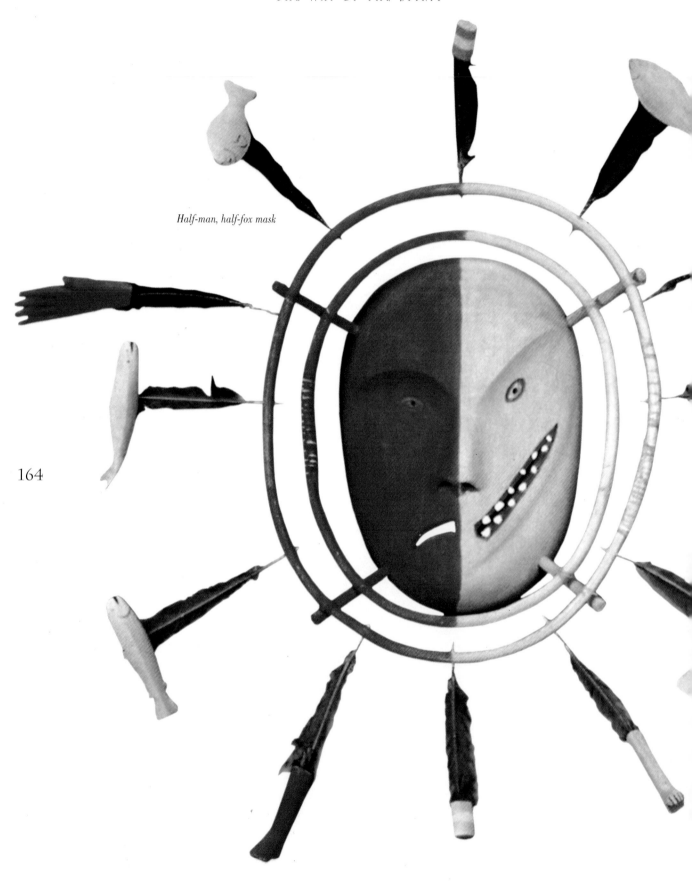

Half-man, half-fox mask

164

GRAFTS OF HUMAN
AND ANIMAL

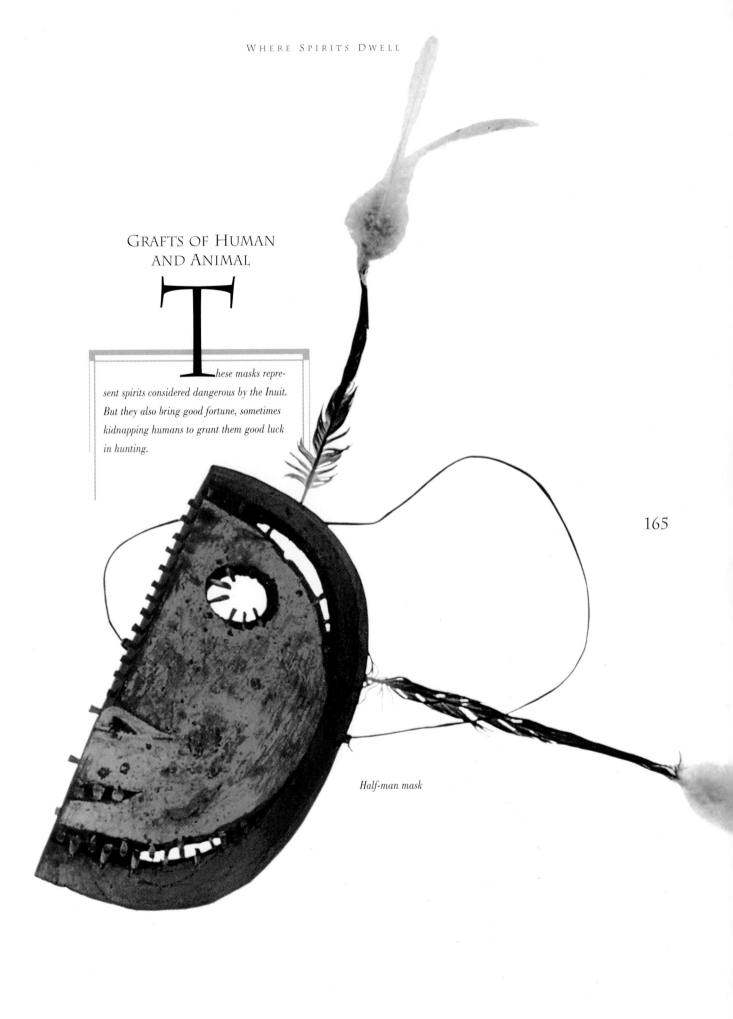

These masks represent spirits considered dangerous by the Inuit. But they also bring good fortune, sometimes kidnapping humans to grant them good luck in hunting.

165

Half-man mask

166

CANNIBAL CREATURE

The bird carvings that compose this elaborate Kwakiutl mask represent the helpers of the Cannibal at the North End of the World, a supernatural creature who thrives on human flesh. The Kwakiutl use such masks during extravagantly staged dramatizations of tribal lore; such performances are central to the spiritual life of many Northwest tribes.

Kwakiutl dance mask

Lenape Mesingw spirit dance costume

MASKS OF THE HUNT

*L*enape dancers impersonating the powerful spirit known as Mesingw, or the Keeper of Game, used regalia such as this early wooden mask with bearskin robe (left). The Cherokee mask of woodchuck hide with pieces of deer tail for ears (below), represents the power of the wildcat. Masks such as these were worn during hunting rituals and by hunters stalking wild turkeys.

167

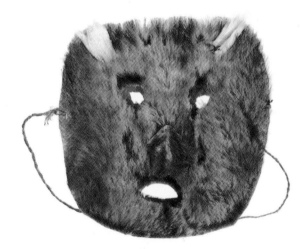

Cherokee wildcat mask

SEASONS OF THE KACHINA

Kachinas are the spirit essences of everything on earth to the Hopi. To obtain the precious water needed to survive on their parched land, the Hopi rely on the help of supernatural beings who dwell in a realm of mist and magic. For half of the year, there is only ephemeral evidence of their existence—in the steam rising from a hot meal or the morning mist hovering over a spring. But in the six months between the winter and summer solstices, the kachinas leave their homes in the cloud-topped San Francisco Peaks and enter the Hopi villages in material form to take part in annual ceremonies to successfully begin the growing season. Though the kachinas themselves are not worshiped as deities, they are regarded as valued friends whose connection to the natural forces controlling rain and fertility makes them key allies in the endless struggle to produce food.

Above: *The Zuni buffalo kachina was believed to increase the number of furbearing animals for hunters*

Left: *Three kachinas observe a solstice ceremony*

KACHINA SPIRITS

During earthly sojourns, kachina spirits dance in celebration of the solstice observances and special ceremonies like Powamu, the Bean Dance, when Crow Mother kachina carries a basket of sprouts symbolizing the miracle of seed germination in the midst of winter. Other kachinas portray powerful spirits like the Heart of Sky God whose thunderheads send lightning. Koshare, or Hano clowns, with their bold stripes, help teach lessons to the children by acting out embarrassing extremes of behavior.

Heart of Sky God kachina

Crow Mother kachina

Koshare, or Hano clown, kachina

THE KACHINA WORLD

T̲he runner kachina, known as Dung Carrier, is said to stuff dry dung into the mouths of those he defeats in footraces. Hemis kachina, thought to bring high-growing corn, wears a headdress of wooden panels painted with fertility symbols decked with eagle feathers and imitation corn tassels. He shakes a gourd rattle to evoke the sound of rain.

Hemis kachina

171

Dung Carrier kachina

KACHINAS, RESPECTED AND FEARED

Masau kachina

Horned Hú kachina

The Masau kachina reigns over the earth and the underworld. All those who use the land are required to pay respect to this spirit, who also controls the emergence of kachinas into the mortal world. The horned Hú kachina with bared teeth and bulging eyes is one of the whipper twins who ritually lash children with yucca fronds as part of their Powamu initiation ceremony.

KACHINAS OF FERTILITY
AND COMEDY

Mastop kachina

Mudhead clown kachina

Mastop kachina, representing fertility, bounds into the village on the next to last day of Soyal, the nine-day winter solstice ceremony, exuberantly simulating intercourse with women he grabs from among the onlookers. The horned runner, Scorpion kachina, is also called Throwing Stick Man, a name believed to derive from the arachnid's manner of flipping its tail in order to sting. A popular feature of every kachina dance is the Mudhead clown kachina, who plays games with the town's children.

Scorpion kachina

WINGED ENVOY TO THE GODS

Birds have long been revered by tribal cultures as holy envoys that carry prayers and supplications to the sky spirits and return with blessings of power and guidance to enrich the Indians' earthly existence. Some believe birds to be symbols of the soul, as well as intermediaries to the gods. Seeking their cooperation, Native Americans have plied bird spirits with offerings and performed dances to honor and beseech them. Pleas are sent skyward in the smoke of burning tobacco. Avian objects pervade tribal life; bird images are worn as personal adornment or as talismans during worship; in the past, they were carried into battle to safeguard the bearer. Feathers are often considered the most potent part of the bird, but beaks, bones, talons, and even entire bodies of some birds have also been used to re-create bird spirits. Many such objects have been passed down as cherished symbols of the power bestowed by those creatures that soar in the lofty realms where many of the gods dwell.

Above: *Bird amulet wrapped in caribou skin*

Left: *Feather bustles and headdress adorn a Nez Percé powwow Fancy Dance contestant*

Steel-tipped Comanche war lance in feathered sheath

*Kickapoo bald eagle peyote
ceremonial feather fan*

FEATHERED FETISHES

The Crow wore ceremonial bustles bedecked with valuable bald eagle feathers dangling nearly to the ground to invoke the eagle's supernatural power (right). Comanche warriors often kept their war lances in feathered sheaths (above). Feather fans are used today to call upon the eagle's curative power, just as they were when a Kickapoo Indian made this peyote fan more than 100 years ago (left). Bald eagle feathers were so highly prized that a perfect tail of twelve could fetch its owner a horse in trade.

177

Crow Indian bustle

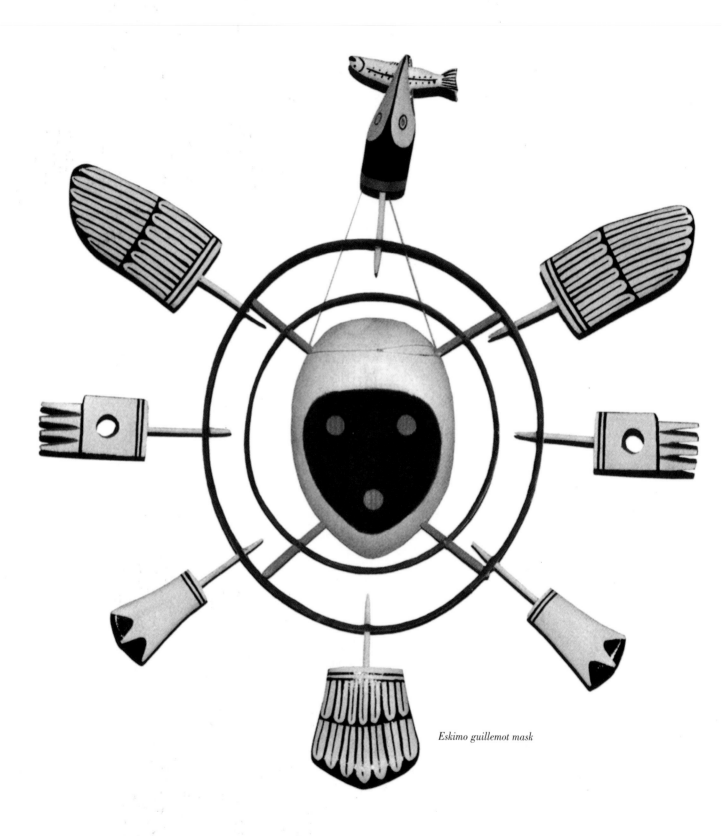

Eskimo guillemot mask

Tlingit prow owl ornament

BIRD SPIRITS

The guillemot is a bird whose spirit is represented on masks featuring carvings of the bird's wings, feet, and head. The mask is worn by dancers at the Bladder Festival, a ceremony held by Alaskan tribes to honor the souls of animals killed during the year and to welcome adolescent boys into the ranks of adult hunters. Other bird images, like this four-foot-tall prow ornament, adorned Tlingit war canoes. Representing an owl spirit, the carving was a powerful symbol of the owner's clan, which traced its lineage back to that spirit.

179

Eagle-feathered Hidatsa war sash

A striking headdress of feathers and a fox pelt worn
by a Salish Native American

180

HONORING THE EAGLE

More than
any other bird, the eagle has symbolized sacred
power to Indian peoples throughout North
America. Because the eagle flies so high that it
disappears behind the clouds, it has been associated with those spirits that are in control of
the elemental forces of nature: rain and wind,
thunder and lightning. In addition, the mag-
nificent creature is held in high esteem for its
physical attributes: Warriors belonging to the
Plains tribes such as the Sioux (right) wore
eagle feathers in the hope of being blessed with
eaglelike endurance, quickness, ferocity, and
sharpness of eye. In previous times, the hunting
of eagles was thought to be a spiritual endeav-
or, and in some Indian communities, only the
most prestigious men were given permission to
participate in the hunt.

The Eternal
Cycle

Working meticulously in the gray, predawn chill of a July morning, a group of young Mescalero Apache men begin erecting a sacred tipi, the *isaanebikugha*, or "old age home," on the tribal ceremonial grounds in south-central New Mexico. The young men lay out the tipi's frame—twelve evergreen poles, representing the twelve moons of the year—on the ground like spokes in a wheel. The main structural poles, known as the Grandfathers, receive special dustings of cattail pollen, whose yellow color represents fertility. The young men first lift the primary poles into position, pausing to acknowledge the four cardinal directions. The first Grandfather, on the east, symbolizes the moon and the stars. The second Grandfather, to the south, represents the mountains as well as the sky elements of wind, rain, clouds, thunder,

Above: *A heart-shaped Tsimshian charm opens to reveal an owl. Wearing the charm demonstrates the triumph of immortality over death*

Left: *Wave cloud over Belly River Valley, Alberta*

and lightning. The third Grandfather, on the west, stands for the animals. Finally, to the north, the young men lift up the fourth Grandfather. Symbolizing humankind, he is always the last to go up because, as the Mescalero say, "man is a frail being," and the other three Grandfathers are needed to support him.

As the work proceeds, a group of *gutaat*, or "holy men," offer prayers to the Grandfathers. The gutaat have memorized the tribe's entire repertoire of sacred chants and song-stories in an archaic dialect unintelligible to the ordinary Mescalero. After the old age home has been erected, the chief gutaat faces the east and raises his left hand. On his palm he has painted an abstract rendering of the sun. He begins to sing, timing his song so that the last note ends just as the first rays of light shine across East Mountain and strike his palm. This is the signal for several adolescent girls to step forward. Each girl is led to her place in front of the sacred tipi by a *naaikish*, or "godmother," versed in ceremonial knowledge. Dressed in traditional clothing—a fringed buckskin skirt, an elaborately beaded buckskin overblouse, and a large shoulder scarf—the girls kneel on buckskin mats,

facing the dawn. Their birth mothers stand behind them, holding burden baskets brimming with food, while their fathers' and mothers' brothers take their appointed positions nearby. The singers bless the girls with pollen to ensure that they will one day bring forth

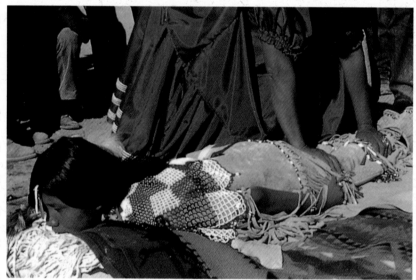

strong sons and daughters so that the Mescalero might continue to thrive.

The godmothers bless the girls and the spectators, and are blessed by them in return. Then each girl lies flat on her stomach, facing east, and her godmother massages her shoulders, back, hips, thighs, calves, and feet, ritually molding her into a strong and healthy woman. A basket, representing the heart of the Mescalero people and filled with sacred grass, pollen, eagle feathers, and tobacco, is brought out from its place of honor inside the old age home. While the singers chant and the godmothers ululate, the girls make four runs around the basket, each circuit bringing them closer and closer to the lodge. The runs represent the four stages of life—infancy, childhood, adulthood, and old age—and reenact the journey of White-Painted Woman, the mother of the Mescalero.

Thus begins the most sacred activity on the Mescalero religious calendar—the girls' puberty ceremony. More than a rite of passage, the carefully orchestrated, eight-day-long event is a reenactment of ancient Mescalero history. During the final four days, the girls go into seclusion with their godmothers and female relatives to receive private instruction about the duties and responsibilities of marriage and womanhood.

What the young people experience during these rites of passage has a deep and lasting influence on their future lives, for in order to begin a productive adult career, every Indian boy or girl needs to establish a positive affiliation with an immortal guardian. Rites of passage ceremonies are the sacred rituals that transform sons and daughters into adults, helping them attain spiritual power, introducing them to the mysteries of the tribe, mysteries not merely of their imminent adulthood, but of all the stages of life.

Above: *Apache burden basket*
Left: *Puberty rite endowing Apache girl with Changing Woman's powers*

185

INTRODUCTION TO LIFE

As the mother holds the baby in her arms, the shaman, with his lips close to the child's face, utters these words:

I arise from rest with movements swift

As the beat of a raven's wings

I arise

To meet the day

Wa—wa

My face is turned from the dark of night

To gaze at the dawn of day

Now whitening in the sky.

IGLULIK ESKIMO

Above: *Kiowa girl's first dance marking the child's entrance into a new aspect of community life*

Left: *Young dancer at a Montana powwow*

Navajo girl   *Apache girl*

Your beautiful

rays,

may they color

our faces;

being dyed

in them,

188

somewhere at an

old age

we shall fall

asleep

old women.

HOPI

Cheyenne girls   *Sioux girl*

Umatilla youth *Coast Salish boy*

The mother and
the godmother
stand on the
housetop before
dawn; the god-
mother speaks:

My sun!
My morning
star!
Help this child to
become a man.
I name him
Rain-dew
Falling!
I name him
Star Mountain!

The mother
throws a live
coal; the god-
mother throws
sacred meal.

TEWA

189

Cayuse-Umatilla boy *Kiowa toddler*

Preparing a Life

The Chief Messenger hastened to the
side of the heavens where lay the Dog Star (as though suspended in the sky)
and returned with him to the people.
The people called to him saying
Grandfather, Grandfather
the little ones have nothing of which to make their bodies.
Then at that very time the Dog Star replied

> The little ones shall make of me their bodies
> See my toes that are gathered closely together
> I have not folded them together without a purpose
> When the little ones make of me their bodies when they become aged
> then in their toes closely folded together
> they shall see the sign of old age. . . .
> And in their ankles and thighs and shoulders (drawn close together)
> and the corners of their mouth and the folds in the corners of their eyes
> the tip of their nose and the hair on the crown of the head
> in all their body from the beginning
> they shall see the sign of old age. . . .

There comes then a time when a calm and peaceful day descends upon me
so shall there come to these little ones
> a calm and peaceful day.

OSAGE

Osage mother and child

191

Cherokee mother and child

192

Skokomish youth

WHEN BABIES ARE BORN

The little Wren is the messenger of the birds, and pries into everything. She gets up early in the morning and goes round to every house in the settlement to get news for the bird council. When a new baby is born she finds out whether it is a boy or girl and reports to the council. If it is a boy the birds sing in mournful chorus: "Alas! The whistle of the arrow! My shins will burn," because the birds know that when the boy grows older he will hunt them with his blow gun and arrows and roast them on a stick.

But if the baby is a girl, they are glad and sing: "Thanks! The sound of the pestle! At her home I shall surely be able to scratch where she sweeps," because they know that after a while they will be able to pick up stray grains where she beats the corn into meal.

When the Cricket hears that a girl is born, it also is glad, and says, "Thanks, I shall sing in the house where she lives." But if it is a boy, the Cricket laments: "*Gwe-he!* He will shoot me! He will shoot me! He will shoot me!" because boys make little bows to shoot crickets and grasshoppers.

When inquiring as to the sex of the new arrival the Cherokee asks, "Is it a bow or a (meal) sifter?" or, "Is it ballsticks or bread?"

CHEROKEE

193

Apache baby cozily swaddled in a cradleboard

PRAYER FOR A GIRL'S PUBERTY CEREMONY

They come to the holy girl early in the morning. When she is thus holy she becomes White-Painted Woman. They also seek out a young boy and bring him there. An old man comes also. From different directions a number of old women come together who sit and pray. Sitting outside, they smoke and pray for the girl, White-Painted Woman, saying:

May you be renewed,

May I live happily.

With strewed pollen may I live happily.

This boy, too, Child of the Water, may he become new.

May I be well.

May I live to old age.

With scattered jewel dust may I live to old age.

May the pollen be on top of my feet.

JICARILLA APACHE

195

Above: *In puberty rite, Apache girl is showered with pollen from the tule, a southwestern cattail*

Left: *Play tipi introduces Blackfeet girl to role of women*

Inuit girl   *Maricopa woman*

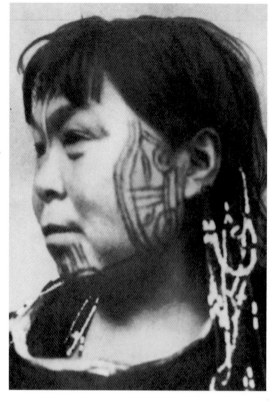 

*You will be
running to the
four corners of
the universe:
To where the
land meets the
big water;
To where the sky
meets the land;
To where
the home of
winter is;
To the home
of rain.
Run this! Run!
Be strong!
For you are
the mother of
a people.*

MESCALERO APACHE

196

Kwakiutl adolescent   *Hopi girl*

Pima woman *Young Inuit woman*

197

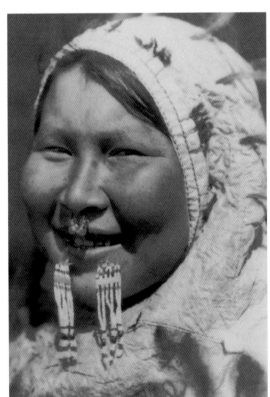

Wishram woman *Inuit girl*

Nootka woman   *Coast Salish woman*

198

Omaha woman   *San Ildefonso dancer*

Tewa girl   *Papago woman*

Sun, we pray.
You know
everything,
You see
everything
on this earth.
Make this girl
healthy and
strong.
Make her
industrious and
not lazy.
Let her have
many children
without pain.

NORTHERN PAIUTE

199

Apache girl   *Apache young women*

A MAN'S PATHWAY

Greeting, Father's Clansman, I have just made a robe for you, this is it. Give me a good way of living. May I and my people safely reach the next year. May my children increase; when my sons go to war, may they bring horses. When my son goes to war, may he return with black face. When I move, may the wind come to my face, may the buffalo gather toward me. This summer may the plants thrive, may the cherries be plentiful. May the winter be good, may illness not reach me. May I see the new grass of summer, may I see the full-sized leaves when they come. May I see the spring. May I with all my people safely reach it.

CROW

Above: *Coyotero Apache wedding couple*
Left: *A Sioux warrior with his two wives*

Acoma man   *Hopi snake priest*

A voice I will

send,

hear me,

the land all over

a voice I am

sending,

hear me.

I will live,

I will live.

202

PLAINS INDIANS

SWEAT LODGE SONG

Crow warrior   *Kiowa man*

Kiowa warrior   *Shoshone warrior*

203

Maricopa warrior   *Shoshone man*

Apache man   *Cheyenne warrior*

We are the stars

which sing,

We sing with

our light;

We are

the birds of fire,

We fly over the sky.

Our light

is a voice;

We make a road

for the spirits,

For the spirits to

pass over.

204

Among us are

three hunters

Who chase a bear.

There never

was a time

When they were

not hunting.

We look down on

the mountains;

This is the song of

the stars.

ALGONQUIAN

Apsaroke warrior   *Nambe Pueblo war captain*

Nez Percé man   *Sioux man*

Gros Ventre warrior   *Zuni governor*

A BOY'S INITIATION

Before a youngster could claim fellowship with the warriors of his tribe, he had to undergo a lengthy initiation. Almost every war party included a few teenagers aspiring to become fighting men. In most tribes, the experienced warriors limited the youths' activities to such tasks as carrying food, spare moccasins, lead ropes for captured horses, and other supplies. The boys were not considered ready for combat until they had participated in a number of raids.

Apache youngsters, for example, were required to accompany four expeditions before qualifying as full-fledged warriors. Apprenticed at puberty to the craft of war, they learned survival techniques and played at raiding games until they reached the age of sixteen or so and were ready to move on to real battles. On their first outings, the boys helped with cooking and other camp chores. It was the only time in the lifetime of an Apache male when it was considered appropriate for him to perform domestic work. The youths were obliged to speak respectfully to all the men, to avoid laughing or looking upward (which would bring down a torrential rain), and never to sleep unless granted permission. Each boy put forth his best effort, knowing that his performance under trial was regarded as prophetic of his future conduct.

Usually the boys shared the hardships of the trail, but were kept out of harm's way during combat. Apprentices among the Western Apache wore a special cap decorated with hummingbird feathers so that they would move fast and not be seen by the enemy. Although they were shielded from the foe, novices were under intense scrutiny from their elders and sometimes failed their apprenticeships; leaders of future raiding parties had no interest in taking along unreliable youngsters. Those young men who passed the test, however, assumed their place among the warriors and were expected to be in the forefront of the fighting on their next outing.

The Kwakiutl of the Pacific Northwest began molding some boys for the warrior's life at birth. A father with martial ambitions for his son prepared an amulet from the tongues of a snake, lizard, and toad, and part of a grizzly bear's heart and forepaw. On the baby's fourth day, the father invoked the spirits of the animals: "The reason I took out your tongues, snake, lizard, toad, is that I want my son to be a warrior, for at the points

206

of your tongues you keep a death bringer. Now you will give this to my son." To the bear, he said, "Let your heart give my son strength and your claws the power to strike his enemy without mercy."

Every day, parents bathed the little warrior-to-be in icy water to toughen him for his future profession.

When a grizzly bear was killed, they boiled the heart to feed to him and smeared the boy's face with its blood so that he might take on the power of the animal. The final test of his suitability for the calling came when the boy was fully grown: He or his father pushed the point of an awl through his forearm, so that it passed between the two bones to emerge on the other side. If the boy accepted the pain in silence, his future success in battle was ensured.

207

A Kiowa boy wearing the costume of a warrior in the making

COURTSHIP ON THE PLAINS

"In the old days, it was not so very easy to get a girl when you wanted to be married," Black Elk, Oglala Sioux medicine man, once commented. "Sometimes it was hard work for a young man, and he had to stand a great deal." Among the Sioux and other Plains tribes, both sexes had to earn the right to marry—men by proving themselves as hunters and warriors, women by demonstrating their mastery of crafts and farming skills. Courtship began with the attempts of a young man to secure a girl's affection, usually through quiet conversation in public. To augment their powers of persuasion, suitors invoked supernatural aid, consulting shamans and other amatory specialists who supplied medicine that would ensure success in love.

When a young man felt confident of a favorable reception, he enlisted his brother or a close friend to extend a formal proposal to his intended's male relatives. A girl could veto any man she deemed unappealing. But if she found her suitor acceptable, the intermediaries proceeded with the details. Negotiations typically involved agreeing on a bride price—as generous a gift in horses, food, and other goods as the groom could afford. In no way seen as direct payment for a wife, such gifts demonstrated a man's potential as a provider and acknowledged the woman's value to her family.

Some couples, impatient with these formalities, dispensed with them and simply ran off together, an alternative usually accepted as a de facto marriage. But unions forged through formal, community-sanctioned courtship were more favorably regarded in close-knit Sioux society, affirming that the act of establishing a family was honored as a crucial part of Plains life.

208

The beadwork on this hide tipi bag depicts a Lakota chief regaling a woman with his exploits

These courting flutes (below) were used to serenade young women
Suitors played magical love music composed by shaman according to instructions received in a dream

TO TAKE A WIFE

Indian women generally married men older than they were. The Tlingit, who lived along the Pacific Northwest coast, deemed it a disgrace if a girl did not marry within a few months of her first menses. Most Navajo women also married in the first year following their puberty ceremony. Among many other tribes, however, it was the custom to wait until the girls had reached their late teens and developed the skills required of good wives.

The marital age of men varied from tribe to tribe. Some wed in their late teens or early twenties. Others waited until they were older. Arapaho men usually postponed taking on the responsibilities of starting a family until after the age of thirty. "In old days, it was customary for a man to marry only after he was quite mature," an Arapaho elder once told a white visitor. "He had to prove that he was a man before he married. He had probably been on the warpath two or three times. Being successful in a war was like passing a character test. He must have had success, too, in hunting and killing buffalo. A girl was ready to be married after her maturity, and after she had been trained by her mother to do the things expected of a woman."

Physical attractiveness normally played little part in the choosing of a marriage partner, but an exception could be found among the Makah Indians of the Pacific Northwest, who valued strength in men and beauty in women. When a young man felt sure enough about his choice for a wife, he would ask his relatives for their assistance in approaching the girl's family. If they approved of the match, his relatives would assemble a collection of valuable items—blankets, clothing, bows and arrows, horses—and send them, along with a respected emissary

210

from the family, to the parents of the bride-to-be. After some friendly tobacco smoking and small talk, the emissary would present the gifts and the proposal to the girl's parents, then leave before receiving an answer. The young woman's male relatives would then convene in the father's tipi for a discussion of the pros and cons of the proposed marriage. If they accepted, they distributed the gifts among themselves. They then dressed the girl in her best buckskin outfit, amassed gifts of equal value to those given by the boy's family, and sent both the girl and the gifts, accompanied by her mother and another woman, to the home of her husband-to-be. A marriage feast followed.

211

Twin spouts symbolize the union of marriage on this Acoma Pueblo wedding jug

COMING FULL CIRCLE

hatever a person's lot in life, age brought some quiet satisfactions. The elderly were generally treated with great consideration. "Our old age was in some respects the happiest period of life," explained Dr. Charles Eastman, a Santee Sioux who graduated from Dartmouth College in 1887 and later from Boston University's School of Medicine. "Advancing years brought with them much freedom, not only from the burden of laborious and dangerous tasks, but from those restrictions of custom and etiquette which were religiously observed by all others. The old men and old women are privileged to say what they please and how they please, without contradiction, while the hardships and bodily infirmities that of necessity fall to their lot are softened so far as may be by universal consideration and attention." But while old people were traditionally accorded great honor and respect, they were also feared by many Indians because they symbolized power and their curse could bring ill fortune.

Elders remained useful long into advanced age. Among the Hidatsa, old men would help train the young through instructive stories and explanations of sacred knowledge, and they made the arrows needed by the men of the lodge. When important decisions had to be made, their counsel was sought. Old women would help the younger women in the garden or with domestic tasks. The time of decline brought sadness as well. But when death did come, it was accepted as inevitable.

Beliefs about death varied widely. Among the Mandan, tribe members could request that their bodies be either buried in the earth or placed on a scaffold—a simple platform held aloft by four poles. The body was disposed of by the clan of the dead person's father. The kin of the deceased would visit the scaffold or grave to mourn for four consecutive days. If the dead person was prominent, the entire village would mourn, and all the fires would be extinguished for a day. The destiny of the deceased was an after-world resembling the familiar one—a place where people resided in earthen lodges, farmed, hunted, danced, and lived in much the same manner that they had known in life.

A Blackfeet couple maintain a vigil beside a scaffold bearing the body of their son and his possessions

213

INVOKING THE POWERS

Remember, remember the circle
of the sky
the stars and the brown eagle
the supernatural winds
breathing night and day
from the four directions

Remember, remember the great life of the sun
breathing on the earth
it lies upon the earth
to bring out life upon the earth
life covering the earth

Remember, remember the sacredness of things
running streams and dwellings
the young within the nest
a hearth for sacred fire
the holy flame of fire

FROM THE HAKO (PAWNEE, OSAGE, OMAHA)

A Pueblo youth listens to a tale told by an elder

Navajo elder and her great-grandchild

215

Cayuga chief   *Acoma woman*

All these heads

these ears

these eyes

around me how

long will the ears

hear me?

and those eyes

how long will they

look at me?

when these ears

won't hear me

any more

216

when these eyes

turn aside

from my eyes

I'll eat no more

raw liver with fat

and those eyes

won't see me any

more and my hair

my hair will have

disappeared

INUIT

Seward Peninsula woman   *Nakoaktok chief*

Assiniboine warrior   *Absaroka man*

*The world is
rolling around
for all the
young people,
so let's not
love our life
too much,
hold ourselves back
from dying.*

TLINGIT

217

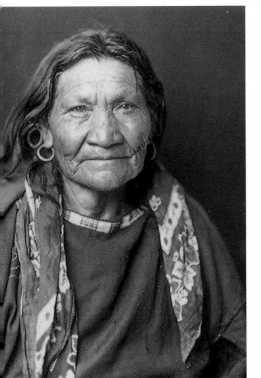

Blackfeet woman   *Arikara man*

Haida woman   *Omaha elder*

*I will sing the
song of the sky.
Now this is the
owl flying
downward,
circling,
tired of all songs,
the salmon where*

218   *the swift current
moves circling,
runs circling.
Their call is
urgent.
The sky
turns over.
They are calling
for me.*

TSIMSHIAN

Mandan corn priest   *Kwakiutl chief*

Osage warrior   Arikara woman

Naked you came

from Earth

the Mother.

Naked you

return to her.

May a good wind

be your road.

OMAHA

219

Karok medicine woman   Inuit woman

THE CIRCLE OF LIFE

I have killed the deer

I have crushed the grasshopper

And the plants he feeds upon

I have cut through the heart

Of trees growing old and straight.

I have taken fish from water

And birds from the sky.

In my life I have needed death

So that my life can be.

When I die I must give life

To what has nourished me.

The earth receives my body

And gives it to the plants

And to the caterpillars

To the birds

And to the coyotes

Each in its own time so that

The circle of Life is never broken.

NANCY WOOD

221

Above: *Inuit woman*

Left: *Navajo medicine man*

INDEX

222

CREDITS

Sources: Illustrations

The sources for the illustrations used in this book are listed below. Credits from left to right are separated by semicolons; from top to bottom they are separated by dashes.

Cover: © Marilyn "Angel" Wynn and © Kathleen Norris Cook. **Back cover:** © Jeff Garton. **1:** Collection of Richard and Marion Pohrt. © Dirk Bakker, Photographer. **2:** © Kathleen Norris Cook. **3:** From *The Way to Independence: Memories of a Hidatsa Indian Family, 1840-1920* by Carolyn Gilman and Mary Jane Schneider, © 1987 Minnesota Historical Society. **5:** © Marilyn "Angel" Wynn. **6:** Smithsonian Institution, Washington, D.C., photo. #772861. **7:** Courtesy Prairie Edge, Rapid City, South Dakota. **8:** © James Randklev. **9:** Colter Bay Indian Arts Museum, Grand Teton National Park, Moose, Wyoming. **10:** Coll. Musée de l'Homme, photo by M. Delaplanche—(painted robe), Glenbow Collection, Calgary, Alberta and Folkens Museum Etnografiska, Stockholm, Sweden. **11:** Field Museum of Natural History, Chicago, neg. #A111349c. **12:** © James Randklev. **13:** Courtesy of the Thomas Burke Memorial Washington State Museum, cat.# 117A, photo by Eduardo Calderón. **14, 15:** Thaw Collection, Fenimore House Museum, Cooperstown, New York, John Bigelow Taylor, Photographer. **17:** © Jeff Garton. **18, 19:** © Willard Clay. **20, 21:** © Paul O. Bolsvert. **22, 23:** © Justine Hill. **24, 25:** © George Goodwin. **26, 27:** © Robert Kyle. **29:** © Kathleen Norris Cook. **30:** © Willard Clay. **32, 33:** © Willard Clay. **34, 35:** © Willard Clay. **36, 37:** © Stephen Trimble. **38, 39:** © Stephen Trimble. **40, 41:** © Willard Clay. **42, 43:** © Tom Till. **44, 45:** © Stephen Trimble. **47:** © Kathleen Norris Cook. **49:** © Kathleen Norris Cook. **50:** © Tom Till. **52, 53:** © Wayne Mumford. **54, 55:** © Eric Haase. **56, 57:** © Eric Haase. **58, 59:** © Dick Dietrich Photography. **60, 61:** © Willard Clay. **62:** Marilyn "Angel" Wynn. **63:** © Marilyn "Angel" Wynn. **64:** © Willard Clay. **67:** Cambridge University Museum of Archaeology and Anthropology. **68, 69:** © Marilyn "Angel" Wynn; National Park Service. **70, 71:** Denver Art Museum, acq. #1948.161; Kathleen Norris Cook. **72, 73:** © Wayne Mumford; Buffalo Bill Historical Center, Cody, Wyoming,

Chandler-Pohrt Collection, gift of Mr. and Mrs. Edson W. Spencer—Michael Crummett, courtesy Chief Plenty Coups State Park Museum, Pryor, Montana. **74, 75:** Milwaukee Public Museum; © Kathleen Norris Cook. **76, 77:** (Ojibwa pouch), Glenbow Collection, Calgary, Alberta, P3205-532 and Staatliche Schlösser und Garten Worlitz, Worlitz, Germany; © Kathleen Norris Cook. **78:** University of Pennsylvania Museum (neg.# T4-344). **79:** © Marilyn "Angel" Wynn. **80:** © Willard Clay. **81:** (Quartzite buffalo effigy), Glenbow Collection, Calgary, Alberta. **82, 83:** © 1995 Brian Seed and W.S. Nawrocki; Peabody Museum, Harvard University, photo by Hillel Burger, #T1908 A.11. **84, 85:** © Tom Till (2). **88:** © Marilyn "Angel" Wynn. **89:** Collections of the Ethnographic Museum of the University of Oslo. **90:** Werner Forman Archive, London/Provincial Museum, Victoria, B.C.—Werner Forman Archive, London; trans. #3820, photo by Stephen S. Myers, American Museum of Natural History, New York. **91:** Trans. #3818, photo by Stephen S. Myers, American Museum of Natural History, New York. **92:** Sheldon Jackson Museum. **93:** Canadian Museum of Civilization, CMC #S91-952 (2). **96:** © Willard Clay. **97:** University of Pennsylvania Museum (neg. #T4-408). **100:** © Tom Till. **101:** Kwakwaka'wakw Robe in the Chilkat style by Mrs. Mungo Martin, Tsaxxis Fort Rupert, B.C., courtesy University of British Columbia Museum of Anthropology, Vancouver, photo by Bill McLennan. **102, 103:** Courtesy The Bancroft Library, University of California, Berkeley; Courtesy of the Trustees of the National Museums of Scotland, Edinburgh. **104, 105:** #A6316, Kwakwaka'wakw Killer Whale headdress from Sullivan Bay, B.C., courtesy University of British Columbia Museum of Anthropology, Vancouver, photo by Bill McLennan; Library of Congress, #USZ-62-52218. **106, 107:** © Tom Till; © British Museum, London. **109:** © Kathleen Norris Cook. **110:** © Kathleen Norris Cook. **111:** © Marilyn "Angel" Wynn. **112—120:** © Kathleen Norris

Cook. **123:** NAA, Smithsonian Institution, neg. #53401-A. **126, 127:** Courtesy Wheelwright Museum of the American Indian (P1A-#8); (P20-#6). **128, 129:** Courtesy Wheelwright Museum of the American Indian (P3A-#4). **130, 131:** Courtesy Prairie Edge, Rapid City, South Dakota. **132:** Peabody Museum, Harvard University, photo by Hillel Burger, #T599. **134:** Fred E. Miller, courtesy Nancy F. O'Connor, © Carnan Vidfilm, Inc. **135:** © Richard Erdoes. **136, 137:** (Red catlinite pipe), Glenbow Collection, Calgary, Alberta, AF 1671; Peabody Museum, Harvard University, photo by Hillel Burger, #T1267a; Buffalo Bill Historical Center, Cody, Wyoming/Adolf Spohr Collection, gift of Mr. Larry Sheerin; Courtesy Charles C. Clark IV, photo by Robert J. Bennett; The National Museum of Denmark, Department of Ethnography, Copenhagen. **138, 139:** © Richard Erdoes; courtesy of the Hafenreffer Museum of Anthropology, Brown University; Courtesy of the Trustees of the National Museums of Scotland, Edinburgh. **140:** © James Randklev. **141:** Werner Forman Archive, London, Private Collection. **142:** University of Pennsylvania Museum, neg. #T4-369c2. **143:** The Brooklyn Museum Archives. **144:** Peter T. Furst. **145:** Photo by Larry Sherer, Dept. of Anthropology, Smithsonian Institution, Washington, D.C., #38732. **146:** Peter T. Furst. **147:** NMAI, Smithsonian Institution, Washington, D.C., photo. #9/3432. **148:** Peter T. Furst. **149:** Hamburgisches Museum für Völkerkunde. **150:** Werner Forman Archive, London/Provincial Museum, Victoria, B.C. **151:** Courtesy Royal British Columbia Museum, Victoria, B.C., cat. #16460, courtesy University of Washington Press. **152:** Peabody Museum, Harvard University, photo by Hillel Burger, #T723—American Museum of Natural History. **153:** Courtesy of the Thomas Burke Memorial Washington State Museum, cat.# 2.5E605—cat. #25.0/215, photos by Eduardo Calderón. **154, 155:** The American Museum of Natural

History. **156, 157:** Larry Sherer, Pueblo of Zuni Arts and Crafts. **158:** The American Museum of Natural History. **159:** Courtesy of the Thomas Burke Memorial Washington State Museum, cat.#1-1450, photo by Eduardo Calderón. **160:** Courtesy Qualla Arts & Crafts Mutual, Inc., Cherokee, North Carolina, photographed by Scott Dobbins. **161:** The National Museum of Denmark, Department of Ethnography, Copenhagen. **162:** The American Museum of Natural History. **163:** Courtesy of the Thomas Burke Memorial Washington State Museum, cat.#1-1451, photo by Eduardo Calderón. **164:** Courtesy of the Thomas Burke Memorial Washington State Museum, cat.#2-2128, photo by Eduardo Calderón. **165:** Smithsonian Institution, NMNH, Arctic Studies Center. **166:** Courtesy University of British Columbia Museum of Anthropology, Vancouver. **167:** Courtesy National Museum of the American Indian, Smithsonian Institution, #2/814; The National Museum of Denmark, Department of Ethnography, Copenhagen. **168:** Courtesy private collection, photograph by Joseph Mora. **169:** Millicent Rogers Museum, Taos, New Mexico. **170, 171:** © John Running (2); Damien Andrus, courtesy the University of New Mexico-Albuquerque, Maxwell Museum of Anthropology (3). **172, 173:** Damien Andrus, courtesy the University of New Mexico-Albuquerque, Maxwell Museum of Anthropology; © John Running (2); Damien Andrus, courtesy the University of New Mexico-Albuquerque, Maxwell Museum of Anthropology (2). **174:** © Marilyn "Angel" Wynn. **175:** University of Pennsylvania Museum, neg. #Y4-367c2. **176, 177:** Panhandle-Plains Historical Museum, Research Center, Canyon, TX—Colter Bay Indian Arts Museum, Grand Teton National Park, Moose, Wyoming; Denver Art Museum, acq. #1948.161. **178:** Maria Williams, courtesy George Smart, © 1992 Sea Lion Corporation **179:** Werner Forman Archive, London/Field Museum of Natural History, Chicago. **180:** American Museum of Natural History—© Marilyn "Angel" Wynn.

223

181: © Marilyn "Angel" Wynn. **182:** © Jeff Garton. **183:** Werner Forman Archive, London, Provincial Museum, Victoria, B.C. **184:** P.K. Weis, Tucson, AZ. **185:** Damien Andrus, courtesy the University of New Mexico-Albuquerque, Maxwell Museum of Anthropology. **186:** © Kathleen Norris Cook. **187:** Dolores Twohatchet. **188:** The Huntington Library, San Marino, California; Rare Books and Manuscripts Division, The New York Public Library, Astor, Lenox and Tilden Foundations, Photograph by Edward Curtis—San Diego Museum of Man, neg. #16059; Library of Congress. **189:** Library of Congress; Library of Congress—© Randy Kalisek/F-Stock, Inc.; NAA, Smithsonian Institution, neg. #56388. **190:** NAA, Smithsonian Institution, neg. #54928. **191:** NAA, Smithsonian Institution, neg.#56118. **192:** © Marilyn "Angel" Wynn. **193:** Library of Congress. **194:** Smithsonian Institution, #75-11740. **195:** Martha Cooper/Peter Arnold, Inc. **196:** Michigan State University Archives & Historical Collections; Sharlot Hall Museum—Library of

Congress; NAA, Smithsonian Institution, neg. #57494. **197:** NAA, Smithsonian Institution, Washington D.C., photograph by Frank Russell, #2629; The Charles Bunnell Collection, acq. #58-1026-2403, Archives, Alaska and Polar Regions Department, University of Alaska Fairbanks—Library of Congress, #USZ-62-64853; Library of Congress, #USZ262-101193. **198:** Courtesy Royal British Columbia Museum, Victoria, B.C.; Library of Congress—photo by DeLancey Gill, courtesy Museum of New Mexico, neg. #59439; Museum of New Mexico, Santa Fe, photograph by Edward Curtis, cat. #144546. **199:** Library of Congress, #Z05200; Library of Congress, #Z051981—Reverend Arthur A. Guenther Collection; NAA, Smithsonian Institution, neg. #76-6644. **200:** Western History Collections, University of Oklahoma Library. **201:** NAA, Smithsonian Institution, neg. #41106. **202:** Museum of New Mexico, Santa Fe, photograph by Edward Curtis, cat. #143715; Library of Congress, #LC-USZ62-97091—Haynes Foundation

Collection, Montana Historical Society, photographed by F. Jay Haynes; NAA, Smithsonian Institution, #1426-A. **203:** Western History Collections, University of Oklahoma Library; NAA, Smithsonian Institution, #42021-A—Museum of New Mexico, Santa Fe, photograph by Frank A. Hartwell, cat. #71236; © 1988 David Stoecklein/The Stock Solution. **204:** Colorado Historical Society; NAA, Smithsonian Institution, neg. #303B—Library of Congress, #Z05200; NAA, Smithsonian Institution, #2023. **205:** Library of Congress, #Z05819; Library of Congress, #216203—Photo by Joseph A. Dixon, courtesy Museum of New Mexico, neg. #68011; Library of Congress, #Z62-83575. **207:** Christopher C. Stotz, Archives and Manuscripts Division of the Oklahoma Historical Society, photo, #3653. **209:** photo by Pamela Dewey, courtesy NMAI, Smithsonian Institution, #30531—trans. #4394(2), photo by C. Chesek, courtesy Dept. of Library Services, AMNH—Denver Art Museum, acq. #1935.193. **210, 211:** Ataloa Lodge, Bacone College,

Muskogee, Oklahoma, photo by Steve Tuttle. **212, 213:** Library of Congress, #USZ-62-48427. **214:** Carl Moon, *Tale of the Tribe*, New York Public Library. **215:** © Monty Roessel. **216:** Smithsonian Institution #952A; Library of Congress—Anchorage Museum Archives of History; Library of Congress. **217:** Courtesy Maxwell Museum of Anthropology; Library of Congress—NAA, Smithsonian Institution, #4650; State Historical Society of North Dakota. **218:** NAA, Smithsonian Institution, #3091-2; Courtesy Maxwell Museum of Anthropology—State Historical Society of North Dakota, neg.#A-1007, photo by R.L. Beatie; Library of Congress, #USZ-62-52197. **219:** NAA, Smithsonian Institution, #54879; NAA, Smithsonian Institution, #76-13369—photo by Grace Nicholson, courtesy National Museum of the American Indian, Smithsonian Institution, #18982; Alex Harris. **220:** Museum of New Mexico, photograph by Guy C. Cross, cat. #1191173. **221:** Jim Brandenburg/Minden Pictures.

224

Sources: Songs, Prayers, Myths, Quotations, and Stories

Ballantine, Betty and Ian, *The Native Americans, An Illustrated History.* Copyright 1993 by Turner Publishing, Inc. Turner Publishing, Inc., Atlanta, Georgia, 1993. Excerpt: p. 204, An Algonquian Poem.

Bierhorst, John, *In the Trail of the Wind, American Indian Poems and Ritual Orations.* Copyright 1971 by John Bierhorst. Farrar, Straus and Giroux and Henry Holt, Rinehart, and Winston, Inc., New York, 1971. Excerpts: p. 49, My Breath Became (Apache), translated from the Apache by Pliny Goddard, in *Holmes Anniversary Volume, 1916,* pp. 134-135; p. 63, Emergence Song (Pima), translated from the Pima by Frank Russell, in his "The Pima Indians," *Bureau of American Ethnology, 26th Annual Report, 1904-05,* p. 226; p. 201, Prayer (Crow).

Bierhorst, John, *The Sacred Path, Spells, Prayers & Power Songs of the American Indians.* Copyright 1983 by John Bierhorst. William Morrow and Company, 1983. Excerpts: p. 95, Medicine Man's Prayer; pp. 98-99, Prayer to a Dead Buck (Navajo); p. 139, Prayer to the Ghost (Winnebago); p. 144, Chief's

Song (Tsimshian); p. 187, Introduction to Life (Iglulik Eskimo); p. 188, Woman's Prayer to the Sun for a Newborn Girl (Hopi); p. 189, When a Child is Named (Tewa); p. 195, A Prayer of the Girl's Puberty Ceremony (Jicarilla Apache); p. 196, A Song of the Girl's Puberty Ceremony (Mescalero Apache); p. 199, Prayer (Northern Paiute); p. 218, Song (Tlingit); p. 219, Prayer to the Deceased (Omaha).

Brandon, William, *The Magic World, American Indian Songs and Poems.* Copyright 1971 by William Brandon. William Morrow & Company, Inc., New York, 1971. Excerpts: p. 63, Navajo: Concerning Wisdom, A Fragment, a statement from Dan Yazzie, a medicine man, quoted in the Rough Rock Demonstration Schools' *Rough Rock News,* Chinle, Arizona, September 24, 1969; p. 95, Navajo: From the Night Chant, adapted from Washington Matthews, *The Night Chant, A Navaho Ceremony, Memories of the American Museum of Natural History,* Vol. VI, New York, 1902; p. 190, Osage: Fragment from the Child-Naming Rites, adapted from Francis La Flesche, "The Osage Tribe: Two

Versions of the Child-Naming Rite," *Forty-third BAE Report,* Washington, D.C., 1928.

Erdoes, Richard and Ortiz, Alfonso, *American Indian Myths and Legends.* Copyright 1984 by Richard Erdoes and Alfonso Ortiz. Pantheon Books, New York, 1984. Excerpt: pp. 130-133, The White Buffalo Woman (Brule Sioux), as told by Lame Deer at Winner, Rosebud Indian Reservation, South Dakota, 1967. Pantheon Books, New York, 1984.

Erdoes, Richard, *The Sun Dance People, The Plains Indians, Their Past and Present.* Copyright 1972 by Richard Erdoes. Alfred A. Knopf, Inc. New York, 1972. Excerpt: p. 202, Sweat Lodge Song.

Fletcher, Alice C., *Indian Story and Song from North America.* Originally published in 1900, reprinted by AMS Press, New York, 1970. Excerpt: p.94, The Omaha Tribal Prayer.

Hogan, Linda, "All My Relations." Essay published in *Parabola,* Volume XVII, Number 1, February, 1992. Reprint permission

granted by Linda Hogan.

Levitas, Gloria, and Vivelo, Frank Robert and Jacqueline J., *American Indian Prose and Poetry, We Wait in the Darkness.* Copyright 1974 by Gloria Levitas, Frank Robert Vivelo, and Jacqueline J. Vivelo. G. P. Putnam's Sons, New York, 1974. Excerpts: p. 46-49, Long Sash and His People, from Alice Marriot and C.K. Rachlin, *American Indian Mythology,* pp. 59-62; p. 193, When Babies are Born: The Wren and the Cricket, from James Mooney, *Myths of the Cherokees,* p. 401, published in the 19th AR of BAE (1897-8); p. 221, I Have Killed a Deer, Nancy Wood, *Hollering Sun,* Simon & Schuster, New York, 1972. Permission by Nancy Wood.

Rothenberg, Jerome, *Shaking the Pumpkin, Traditional Poetry of the Indian North Americas.* Copyright 1972 by Jerome Rothenberg. Doubleday & Company, Inc., New York. Permission by Jerome Rothenberg and Armand Schwerner (translator). Excerpt: p. 216, Song of the Old Woman (Eskimo).